MAY - 2024

dabble lab

Manga Drawing with

HOW TO DRAW DC SUPER-PETS MANGA!

by Christopher Harbo

illustrated by Mel Joy San Juan
cover artwork by Haining

CAPSTONE PRESS
a capstone imprint

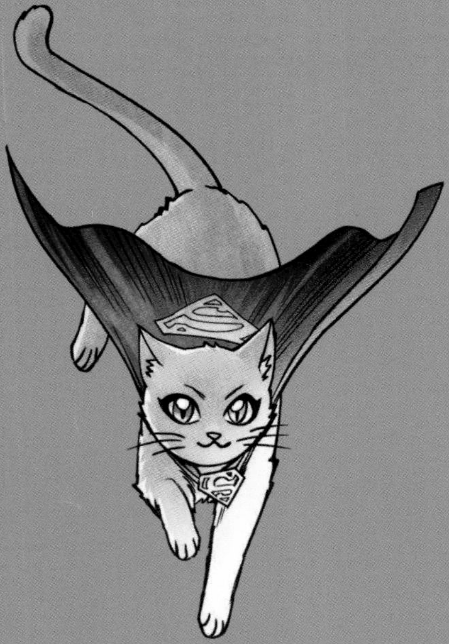

Published by Capstone Press, an imprint of Capstone.
1710 Roe Crest Drive
North Mankato, Minnesota 56003
capstonepub.com

Library of Congress Cataloging-in-Publication Data
is available on the Library of Congress website.
ISBN: 9781669021636 (hardcover)
ISBN: 9781669021599 (ebook PDF)

Summary: DC Super-Pets and manga unite! Put a new spin on furry Super Heroes and Super-Villains, and learn to draw them as dynamic manga characters with easy-to-follow steps.

Editorial Credits
Editor: Abby Huff; Designer: Hilary Wacholz;
Media Researcher: Jo Miller; Production Specialist: Tori Abraham

Image Credits
Photos: Capstone Studio: Karon Dubke 5 (all), Backgrounds and design elements: Capstone

Printed in the United States 5789

TABLE OF CONTENTS

THE MAGIC OF MANGA!

Believe it or not, Super-Pets have been helping Super Heroes curb crime for more than 80 years. Wonder Woman had the very first pet when Jumpa the Kanga leaped onto the scene in 1942. But Batman and Superman weren't about to be left in the dust. Soon they were battling baddies with Ace the Bat-Hound and Krypto the Super-Dog. In time, a whole Legion of Super-Pets formed. The world has been a little friendlier, and furrier, ever since!

While Super-Pets were starting to save the day in American comics in the 1940s, the magic of manga was sweeping Japan. These comics and graphic novels have gone on to dazzle fans worldwide. Manga is famous for its dynamic human characters with large eyes, small noses and mouths, and pointed chins. But animals have also starred in many manga adventures of their own. Cats, dogs, dinosaurs, unicorns . . . nearly every kind of critter has populated the pages of Japanese comics.

SO WHAT ARE YOU WAITING FOR? IT'S TIME TO BRING THE MAGIC OF MANGA TO THE POWERFUL PETS OF THE DC UNIVERSE. YOU'RE ABOUT TO DRAW THE DC SUPER-PETS IN MANGA STYLE!

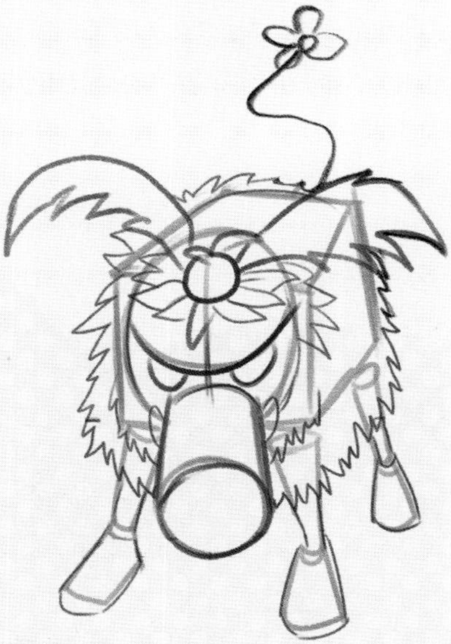

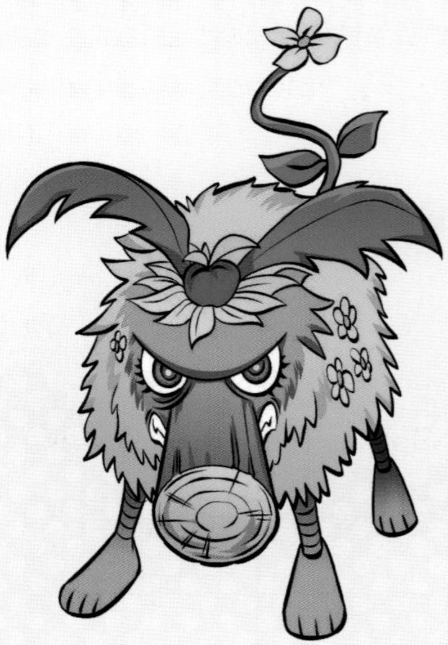

THE MANGAKA'S TOOLKIT

All manga artists—or mangaka—need the right tools to make amazing art. Gather the following supplies before you begin drawing:

PAPER

Art supply and hobby stores have many types of special drawing paper. But any blank, unlined paper will work well too.

PENCILS

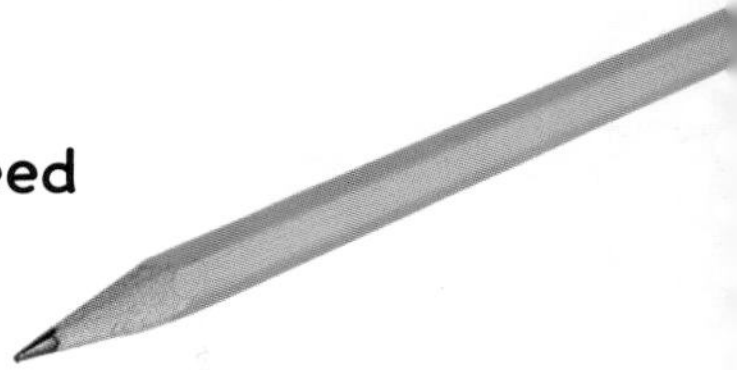

Sketch in pencil first. That way, if you make a mistake or need to change a detail, it's easy to erase and redraw.

PENCIL SHARPENER

Keep a good pencil sharpener within reach. Sharp pencils will help you draw clean lines.

ERASERS

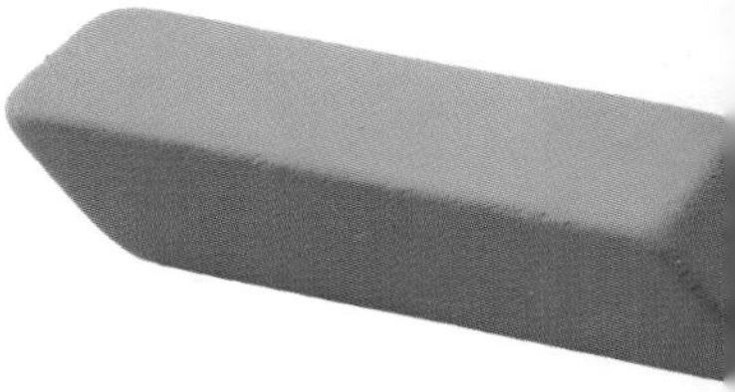

Making mistakes is a normal part of drawing. Regular pencil erasers work in a pinch. But high-quality rubber or kneaded erasers last longer and won't damage your paper.

BLACK MARKER PENS

When your sketch is done, trace over the final lines with a black marker pen. By "inking" the lines, your characters will practically leap off the page!

COLORED PENCILS AND MARKERS

While manga stories are usually created in black and white, they often have full-color covers. Feel free to complete your manga masterpiece with colored pencils and markers. There's nothing like a pop of color to bring characters to life!

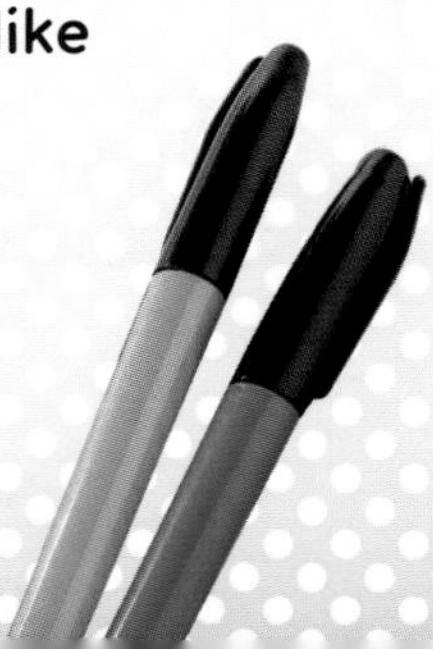

KRYPTO

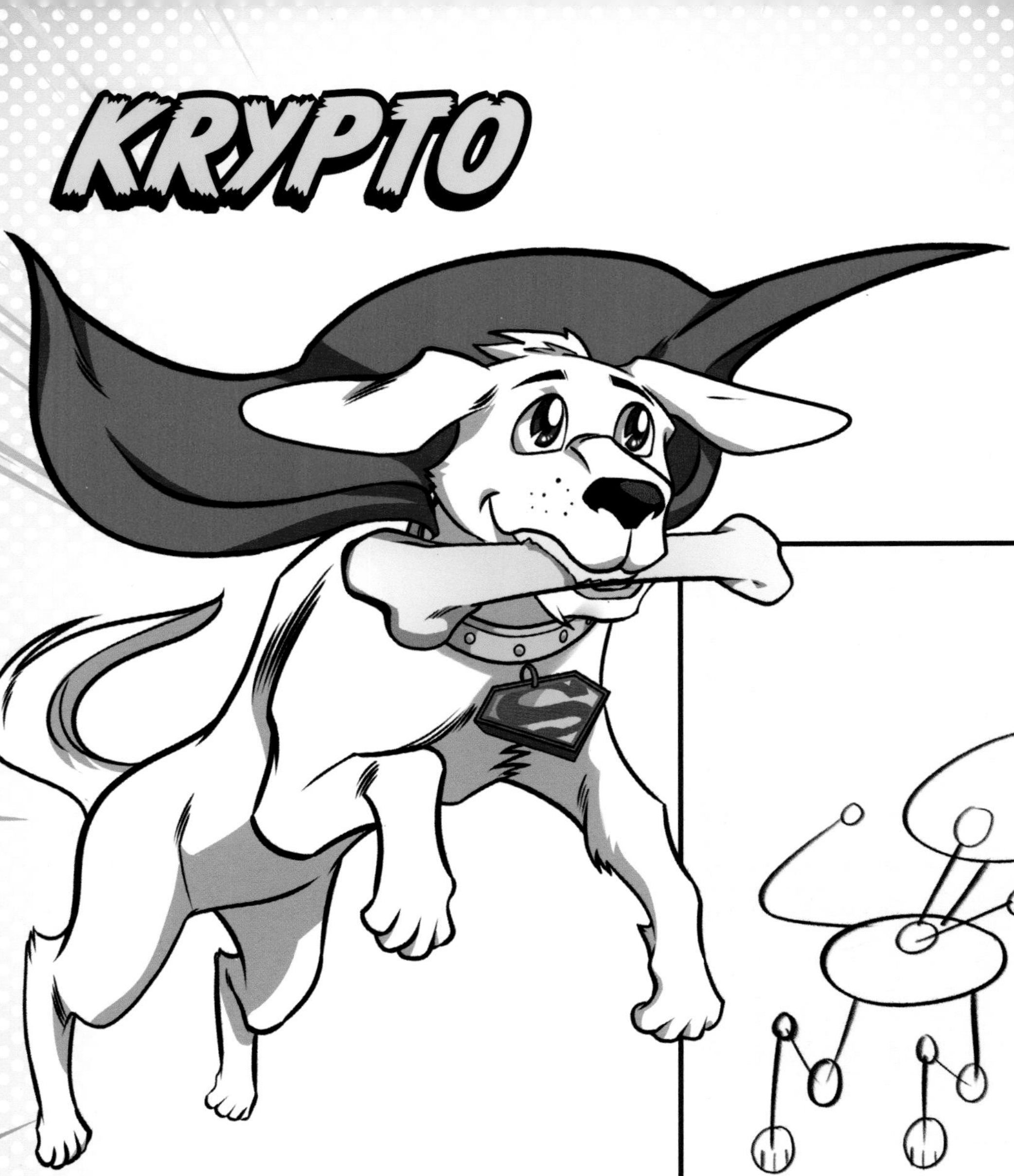

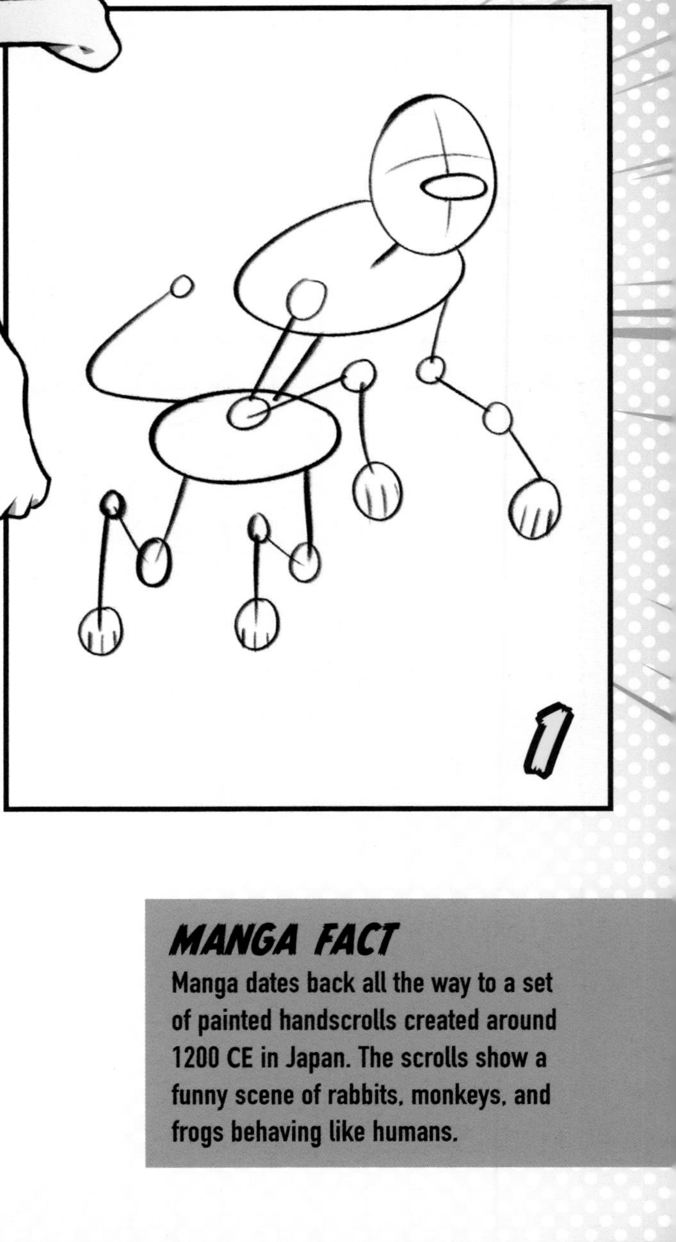
1

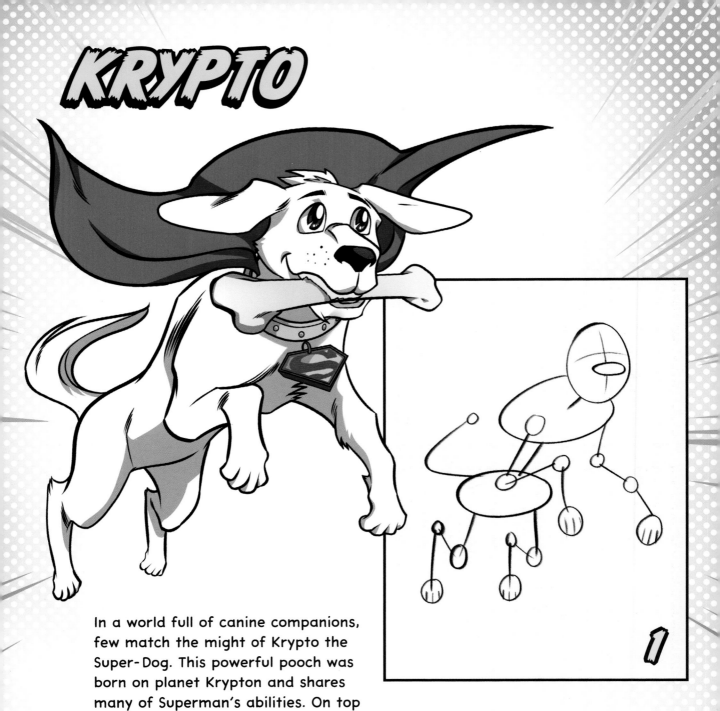

In a world full of canine companions, few match the might of Krypto the Super-Dog. This powerful pooch was born on planet Krypton and shares many of Superman's abilities. On top of super-strength and X-ray vision, Krypto also has souped-up senses of smell and hearing. So whenever the Man of Steel sends out a supersonic whistle, the Dog of Steel swiftly soars to his best friend's side!

MANGA FACT

Manga dates back all the way to a set of painted handscrolls created around 1200 CE in Japan. The scrolls show a funny scene of rabbits, monkeys, and frogs behaving like humans.

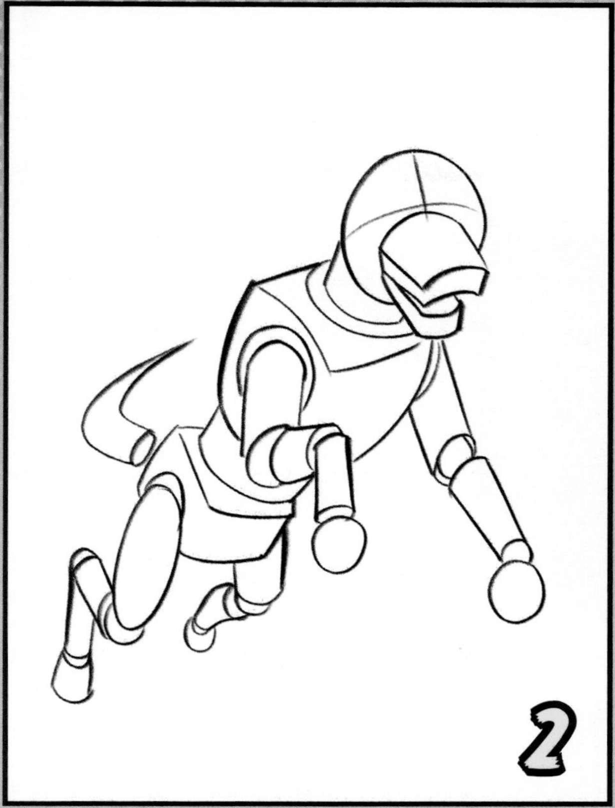
2
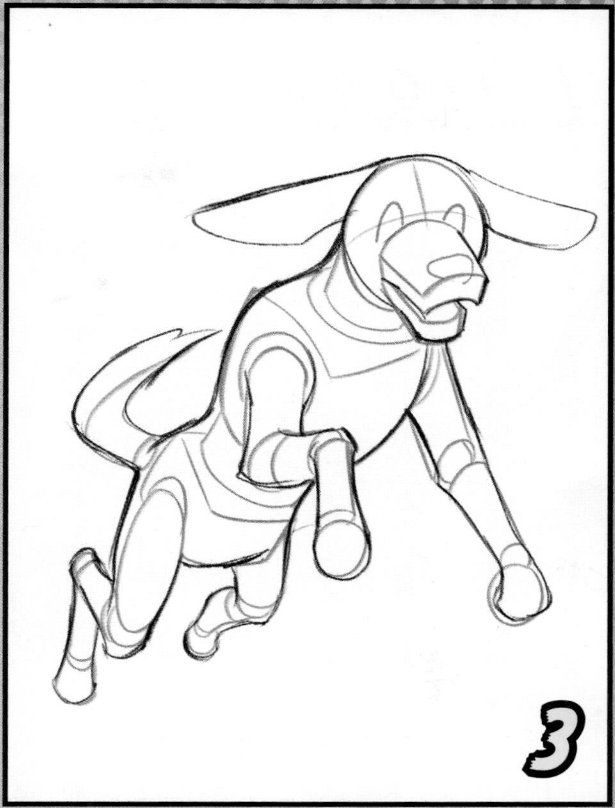
3
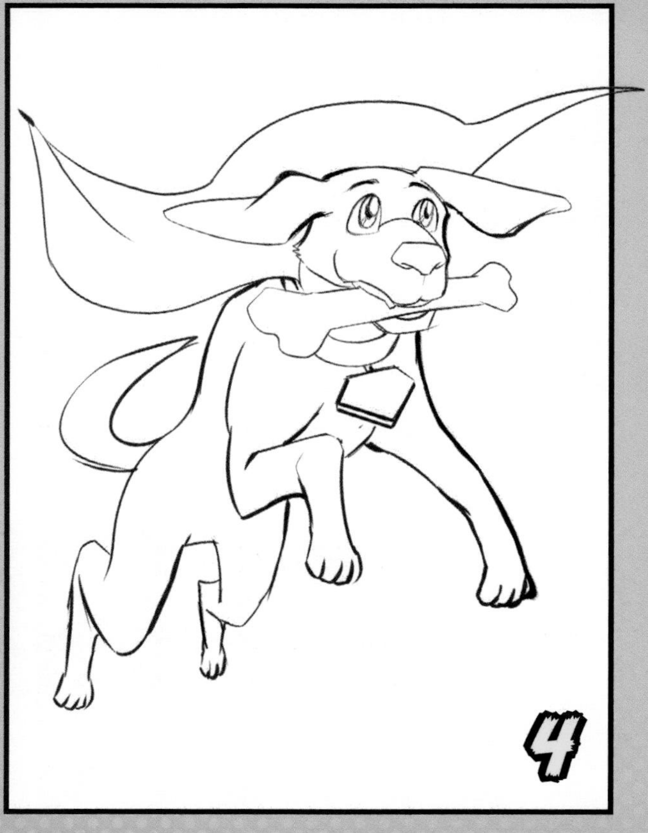
4
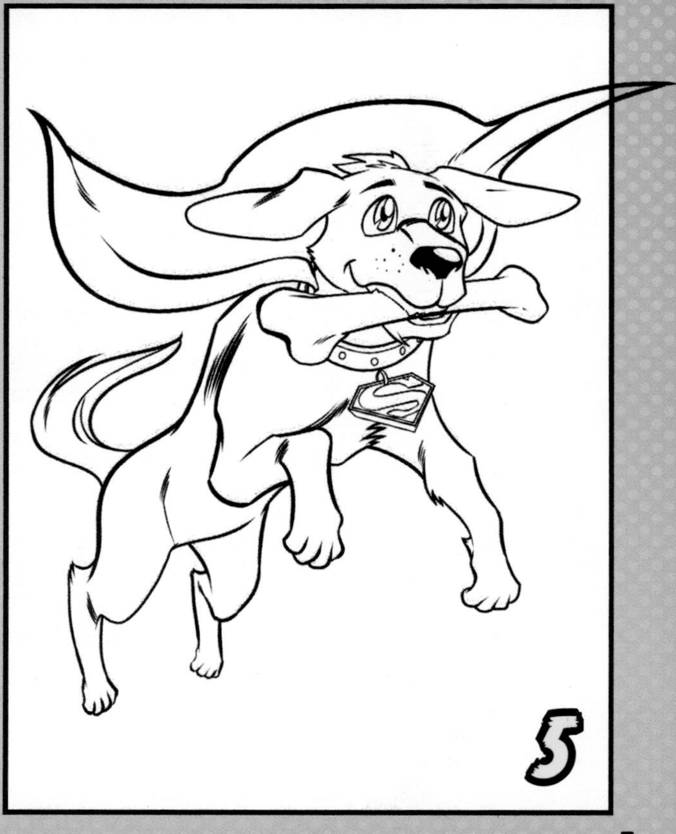
5

ACE

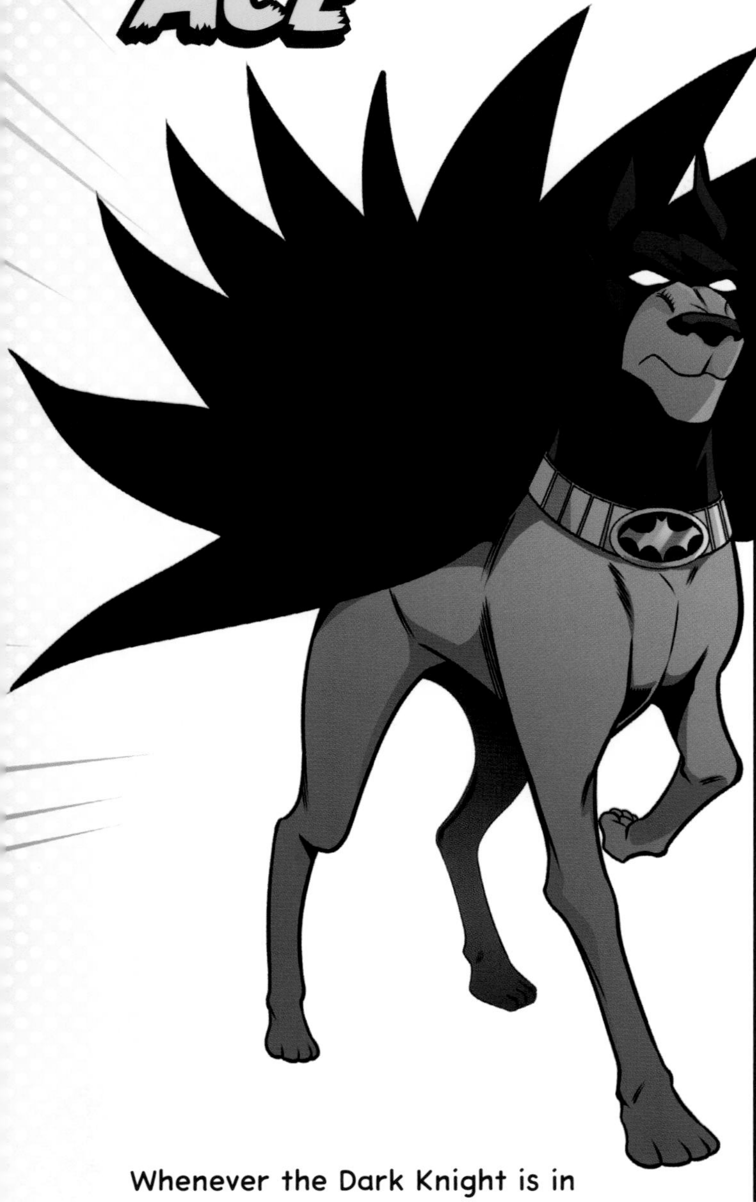

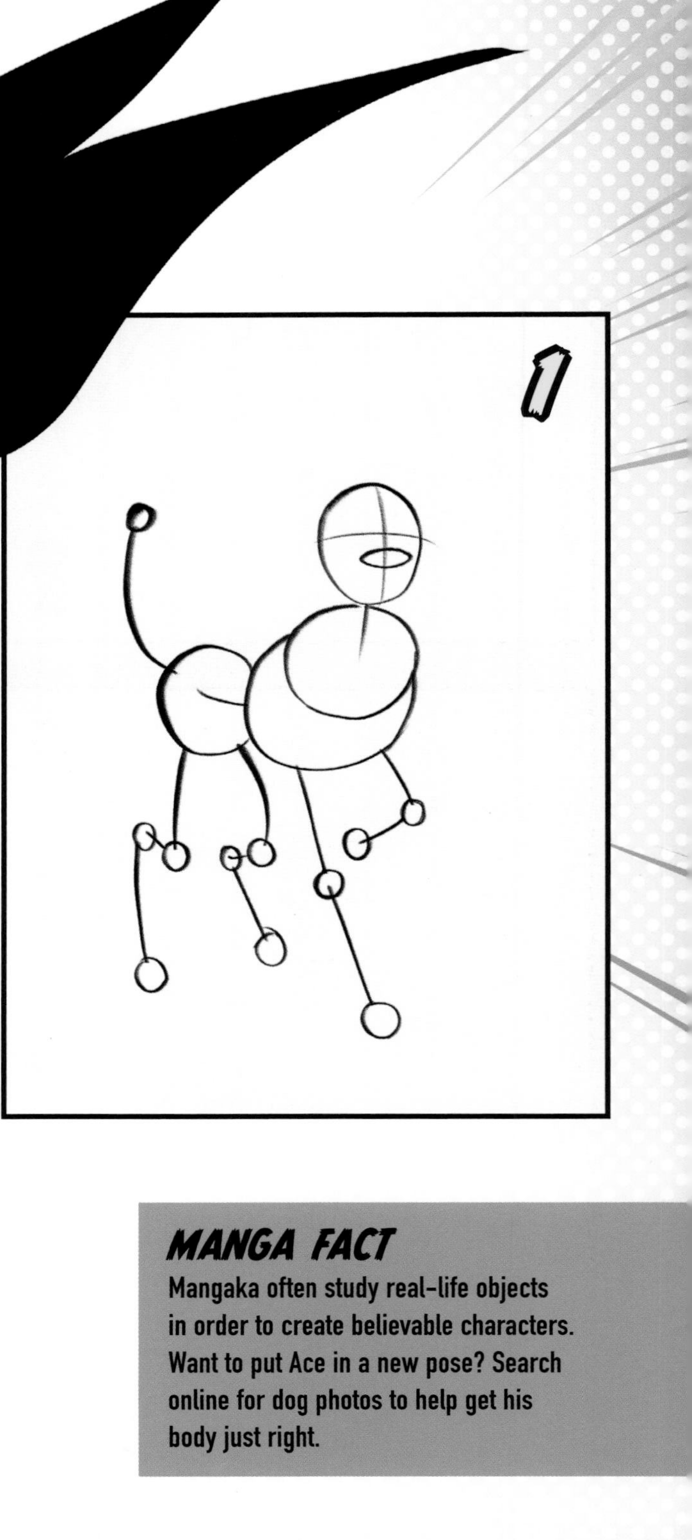
1

Whenever the Dark Knight is in danger, Ace the Bat-Hound has his back. This canine crime fighter isn't afraid to face a *ruff* crowd. But his most *scent*-sational ability? A nose for finding ne'er-do-wells up to no good. With this sleuthing skill, Ace proves time and again that he's the perfect pal for Batman, the World's Greatest Detective.

MANGA FACT

Mangaka often study real-life objects in order to create believable characters. Want to put Ace in a new pose? Search online for dog photos to help get his body just right.

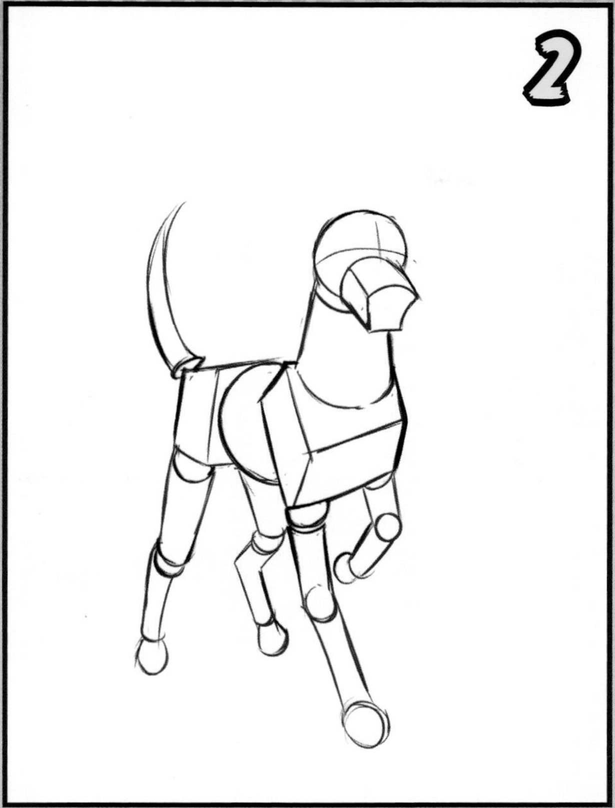
2
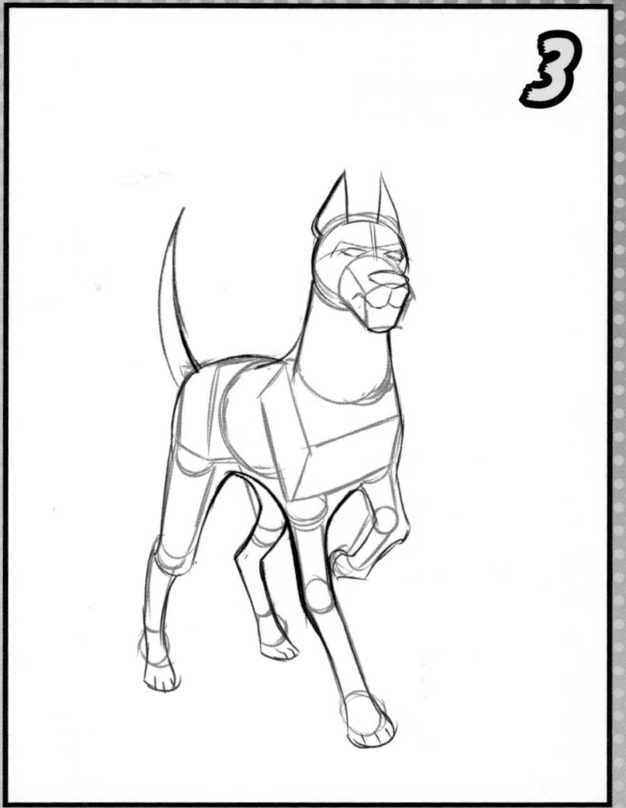
3
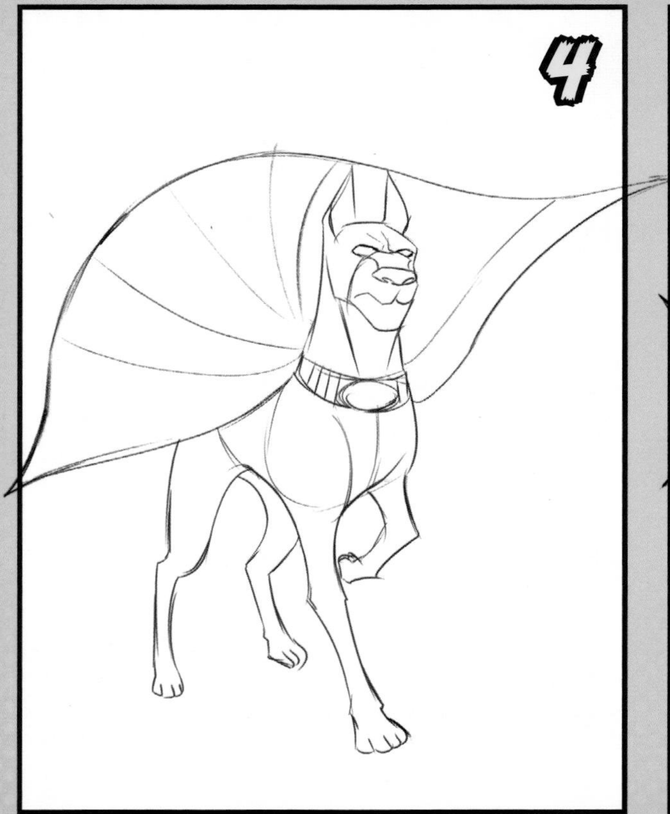
4
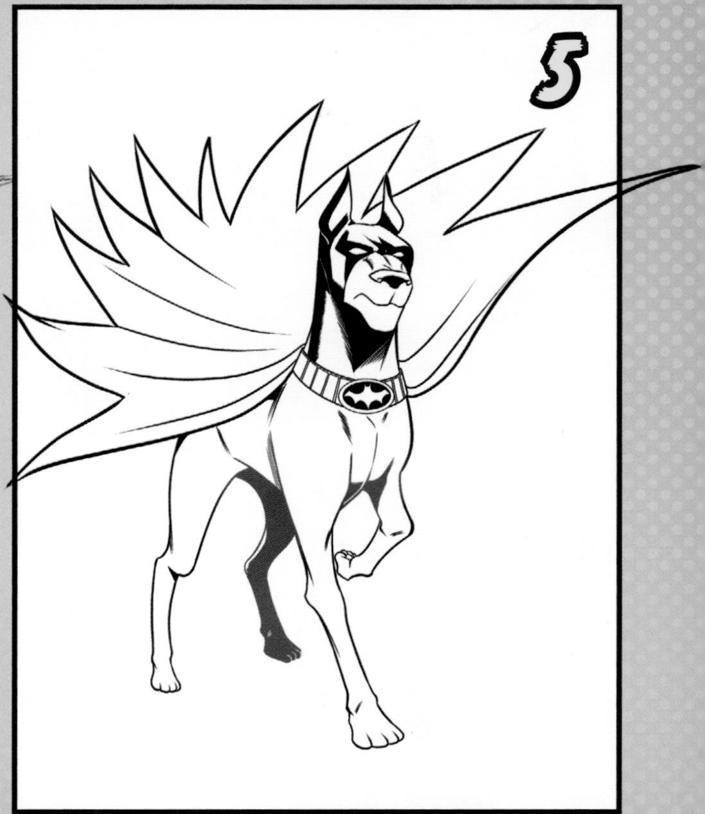
5

JUMPA

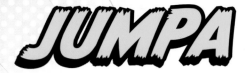

Every warrior princess needs a royal steed—and Wonder Woman is no exception. Luckily, the Amazing Amazon can saddle up Jumpa whenever she has a need for speed. This giant Kanga is a swift runner and powerful jumper. Whether running races on Paradise Island or leaping into battle, Jumpa is ready to spring into action!

MANGA FACT

Some manga animals are drawn with lifelike proportions. Others are stylized, with large heads and short legs. Play with your art style to see which you like best!

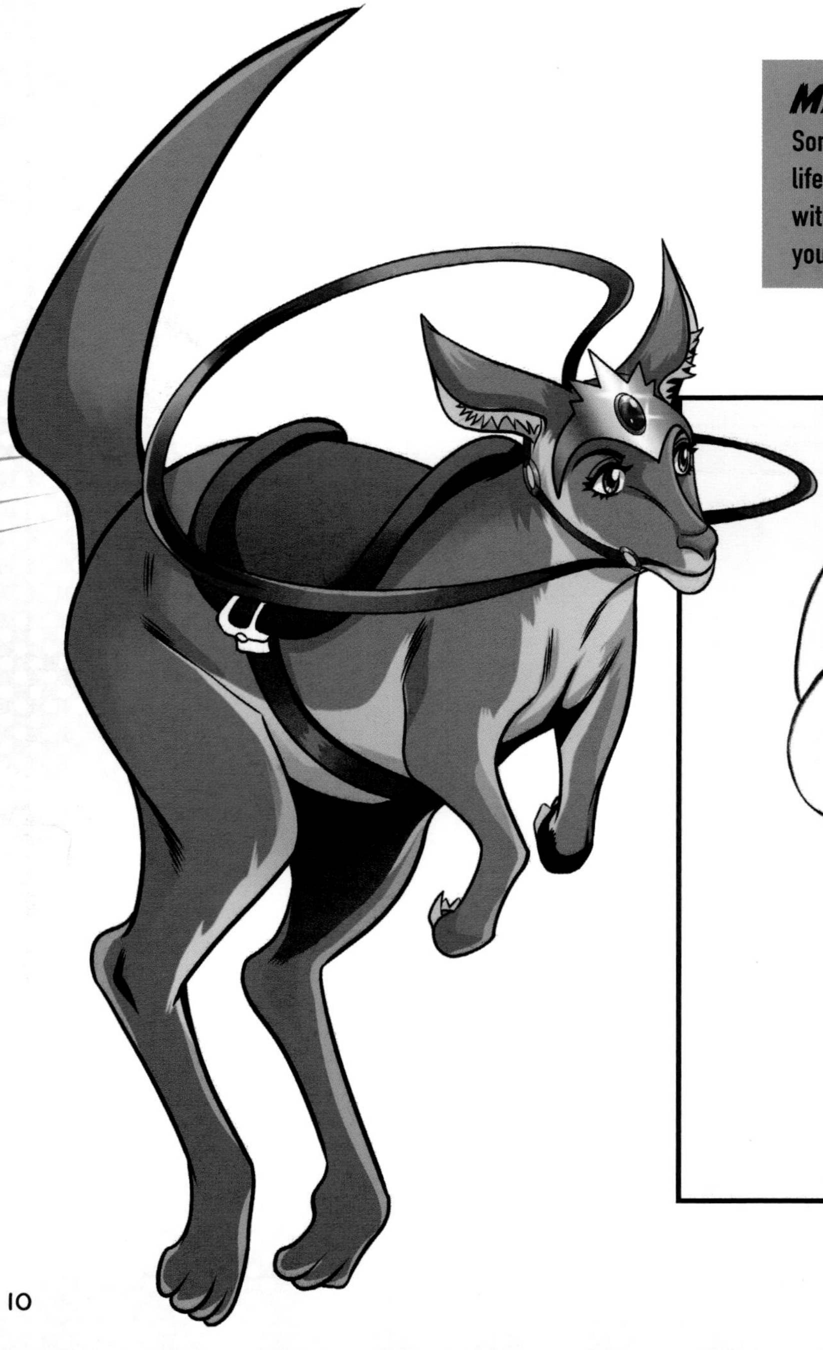

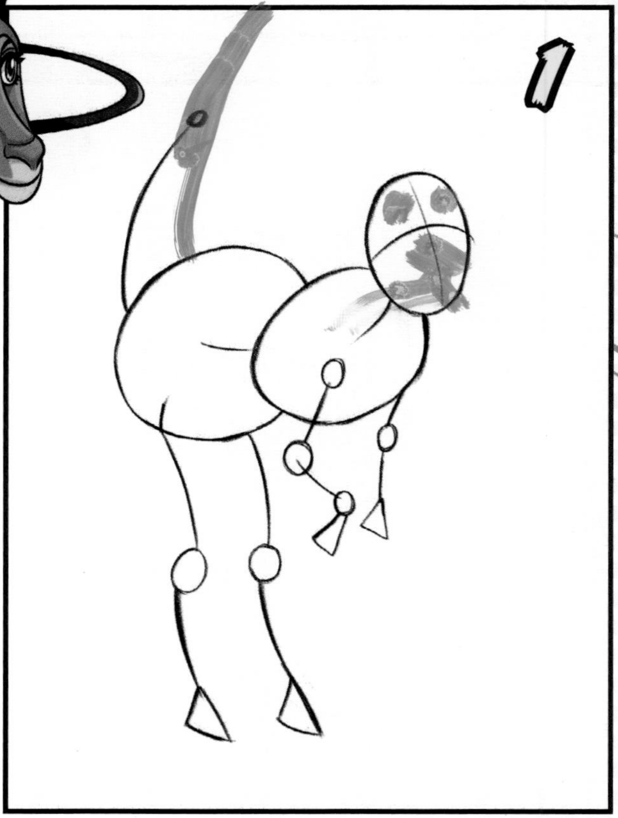
1

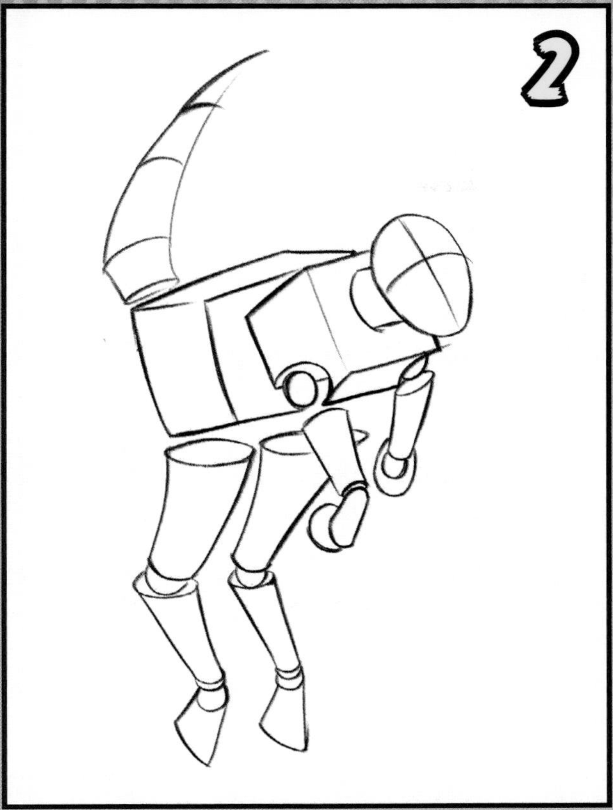
2
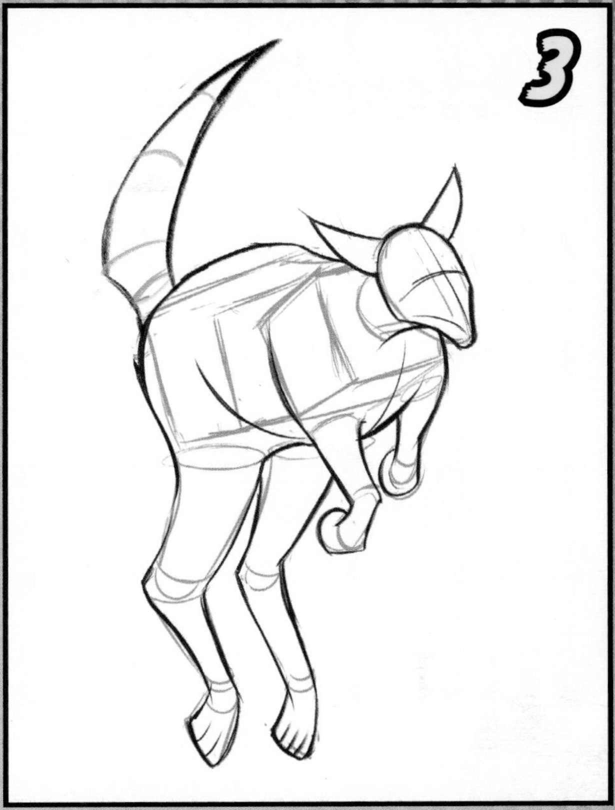
3
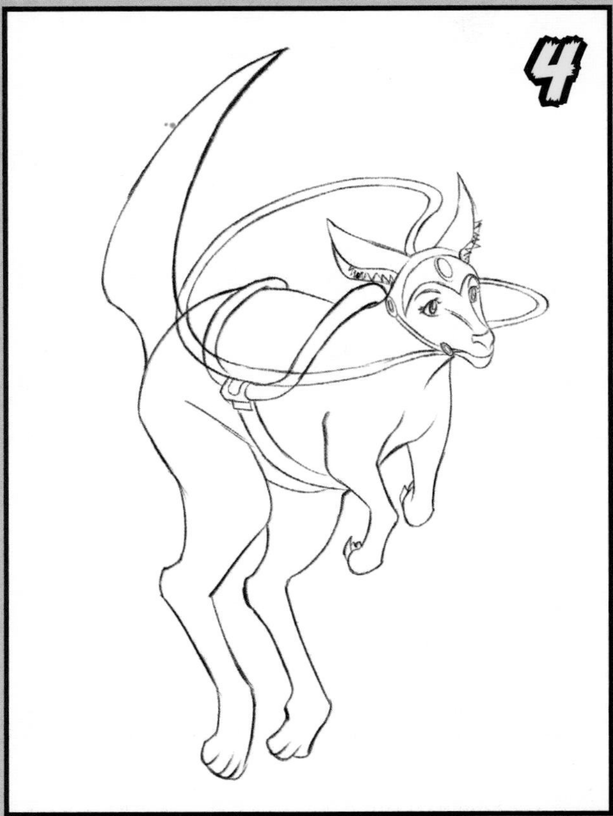
4
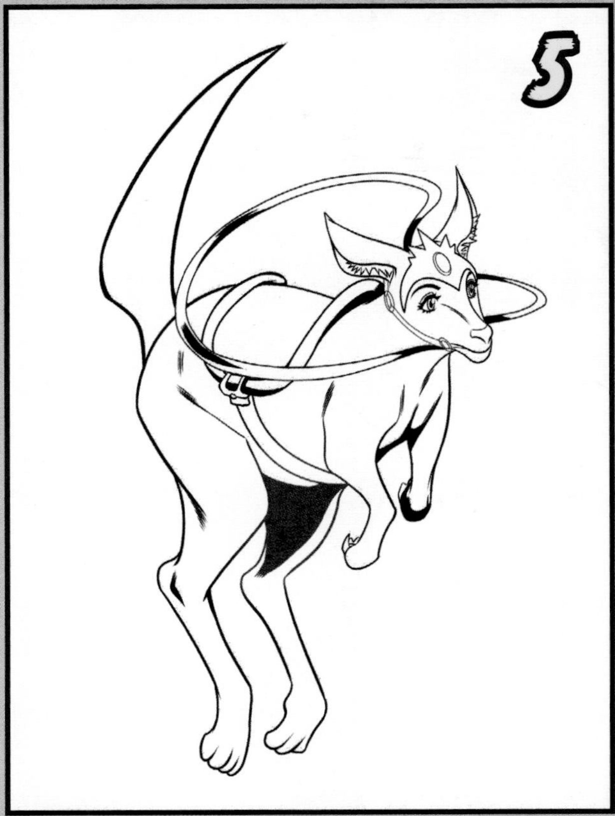
5

STREAKY

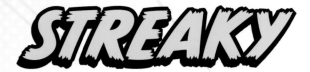

Streaky started out as Supergirl's normal pet cat. Then an experiment with X-Kryptonite changed everything! The radioactive rock gave Streaky *paw*-some superpowers. Heat vision, super-strength, super-speed, and flight are all at the command of this fearless feline. Now the Super-Cat dons a cape and S-Shield anytime he takes a swipe at a Super-Villain!

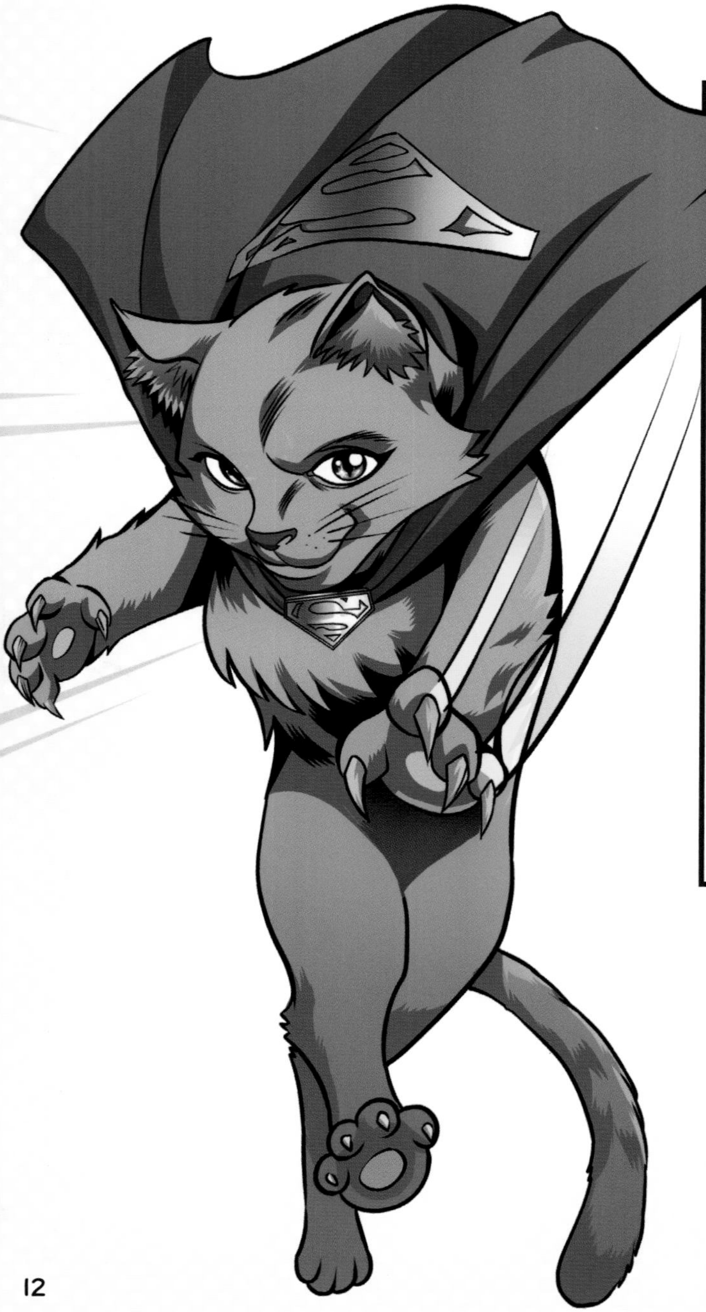

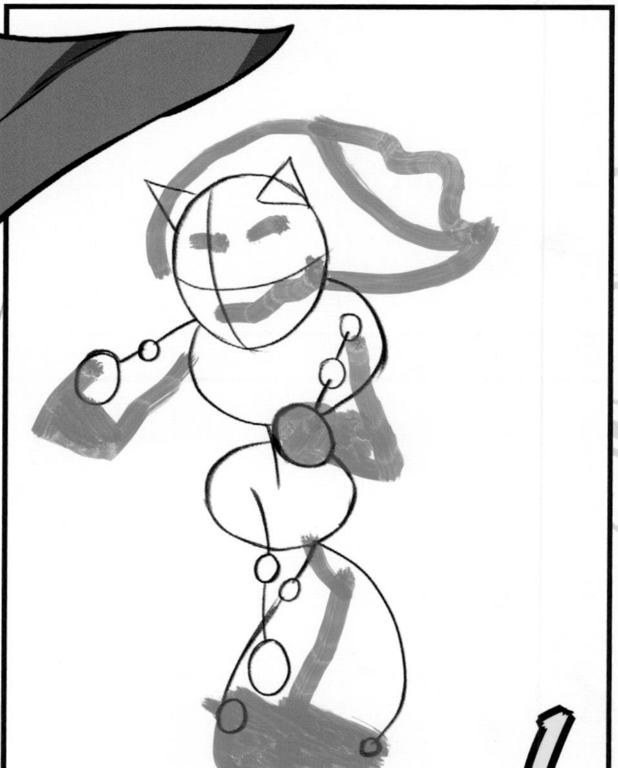
1

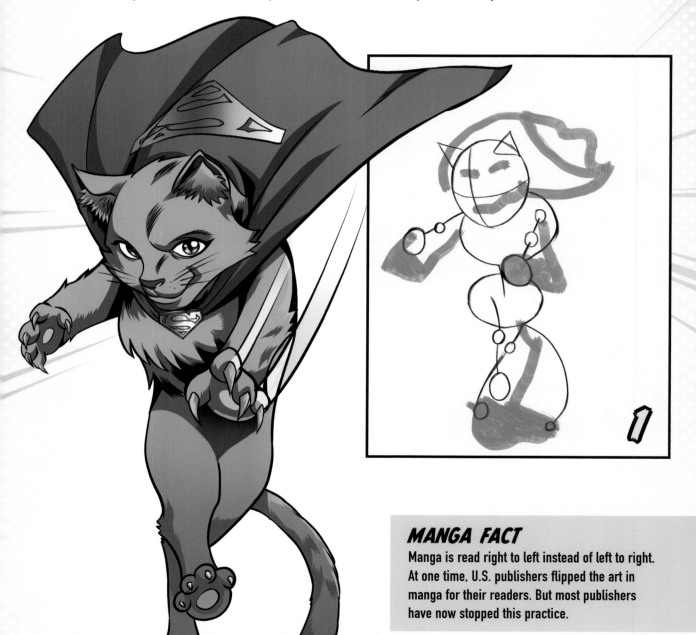

MANGA FACT

Manga is read right to left instead of left to right. At one time, U.S. publishers flipped the art in manga for their readers. But most publishers have now stopped this practice.

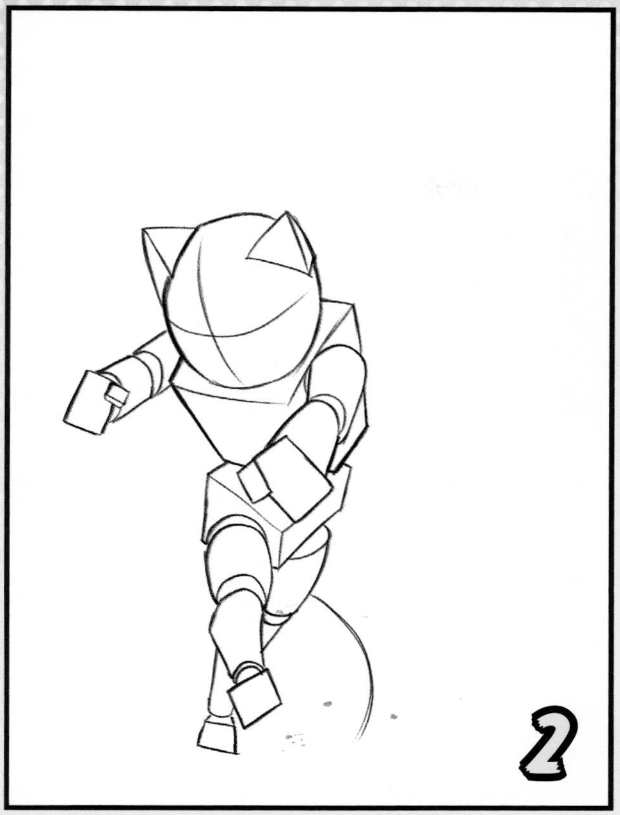
2
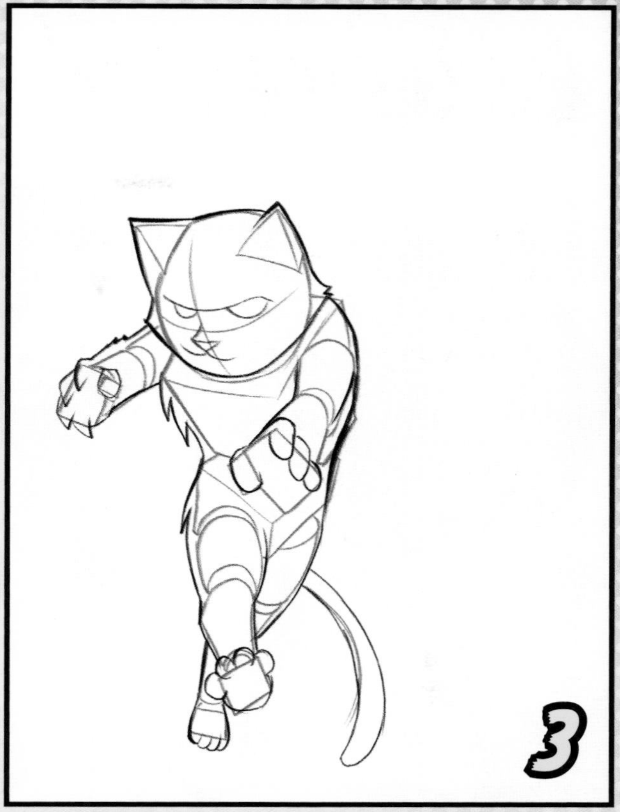
3
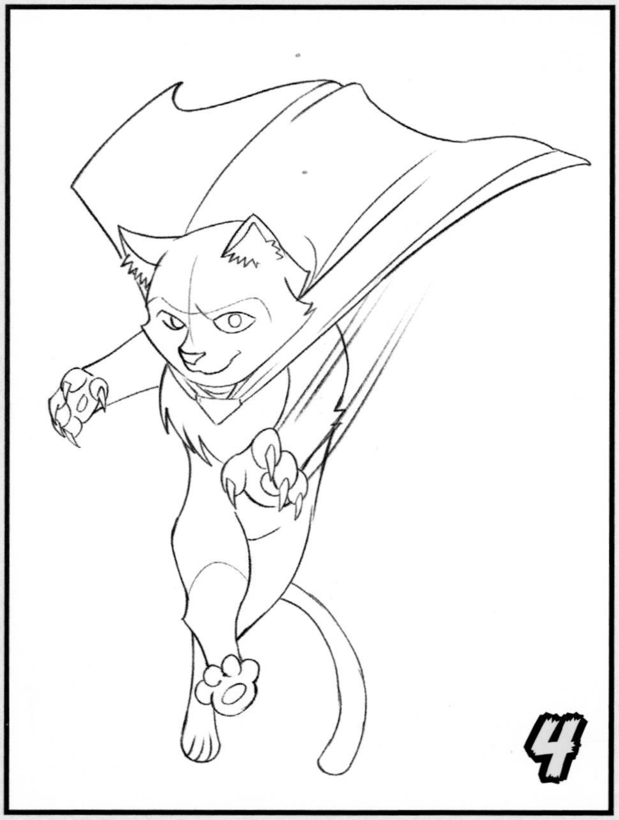
4
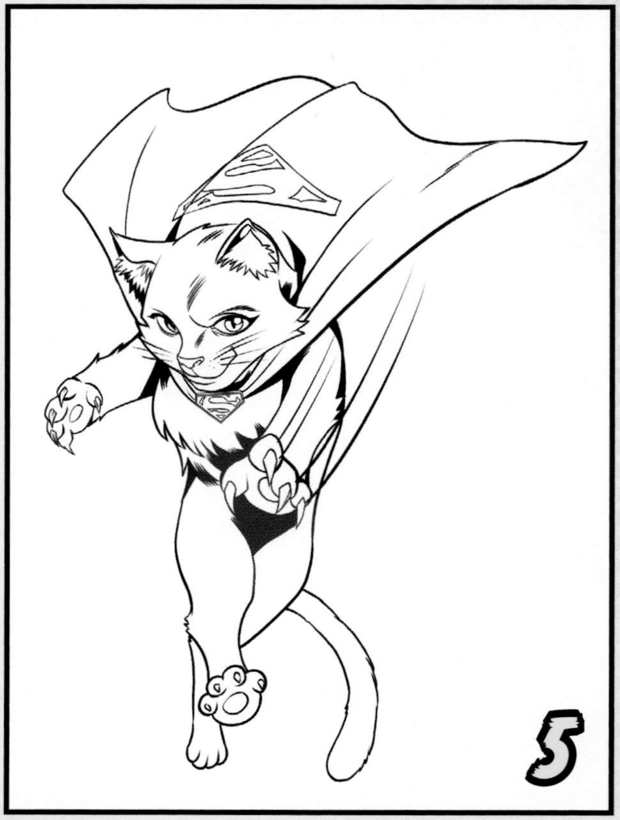
5

COMET

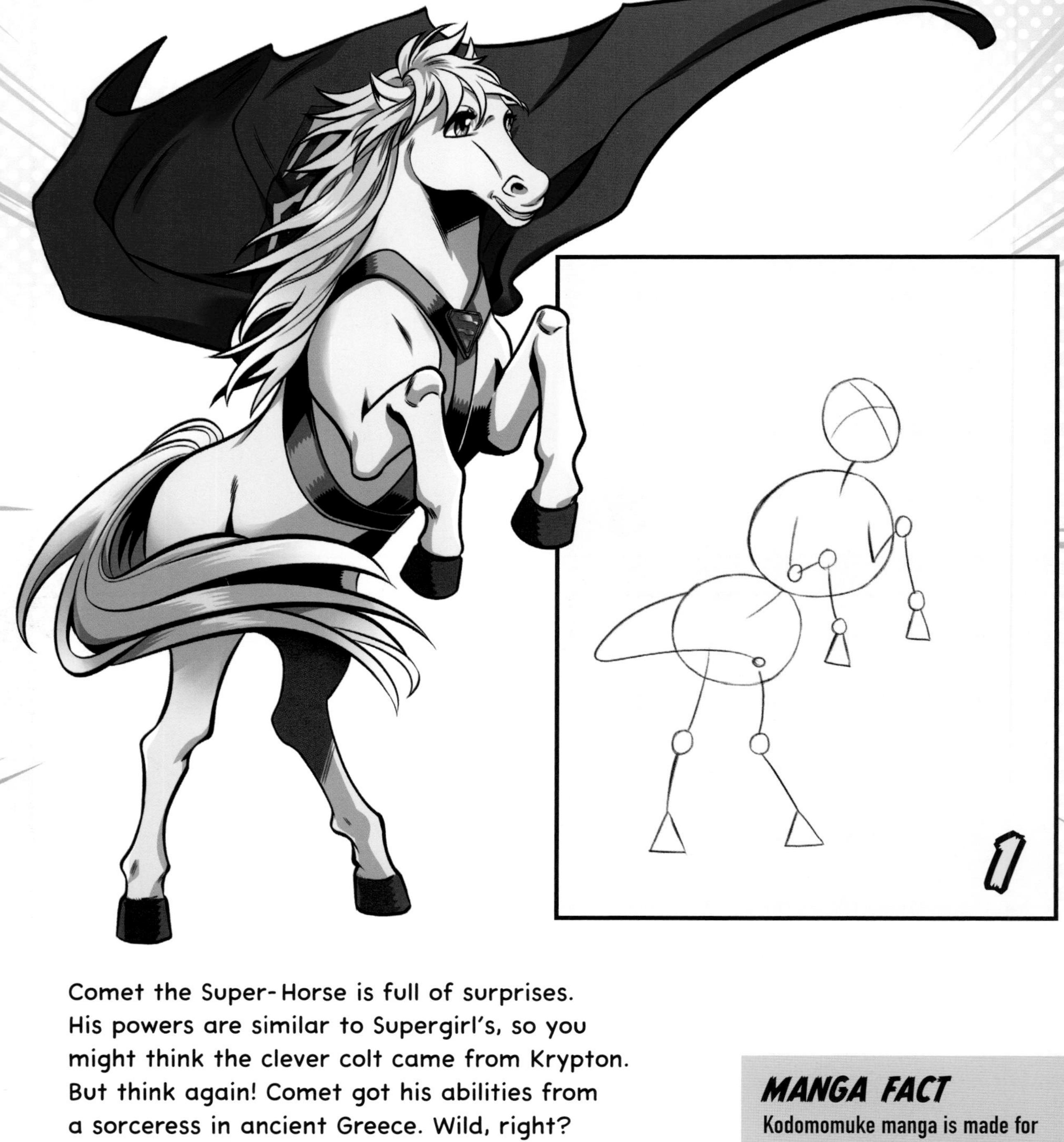
1

Comet the Super-Horse is full of surprises. His powers are similar to Supergirl's, so you might think the clever colt came from Krypton. But think again! Comet got his abilities from a sorceress in ancient Greece. Wild, right? Even more astonishing is his ability to speak to the Girl of Steel with his mind! Whoa, Nelly! Talk about a super-steed indeed.

MANGA FACT

Kodomomuke manga is made for younger readers. These series often have fun stories with cute characters and moral lessons. *Pokémon* is a popular kodomomuke series.

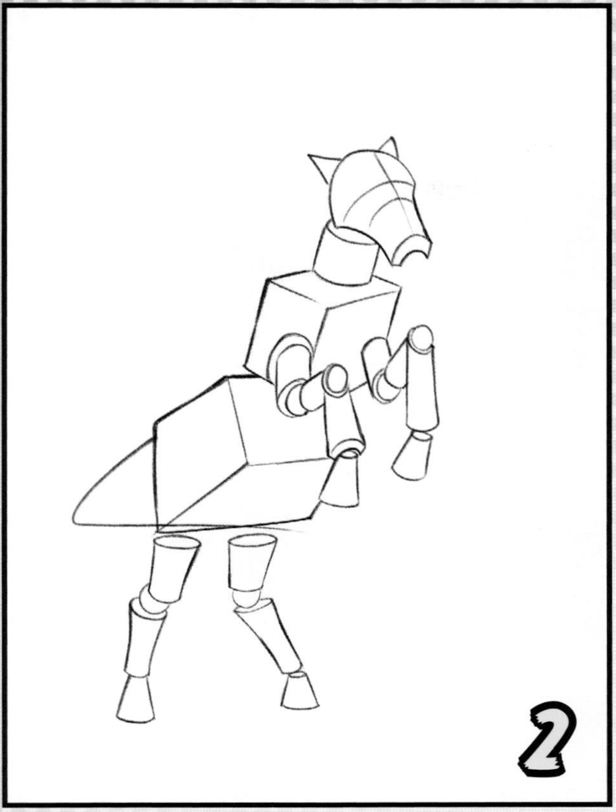
2
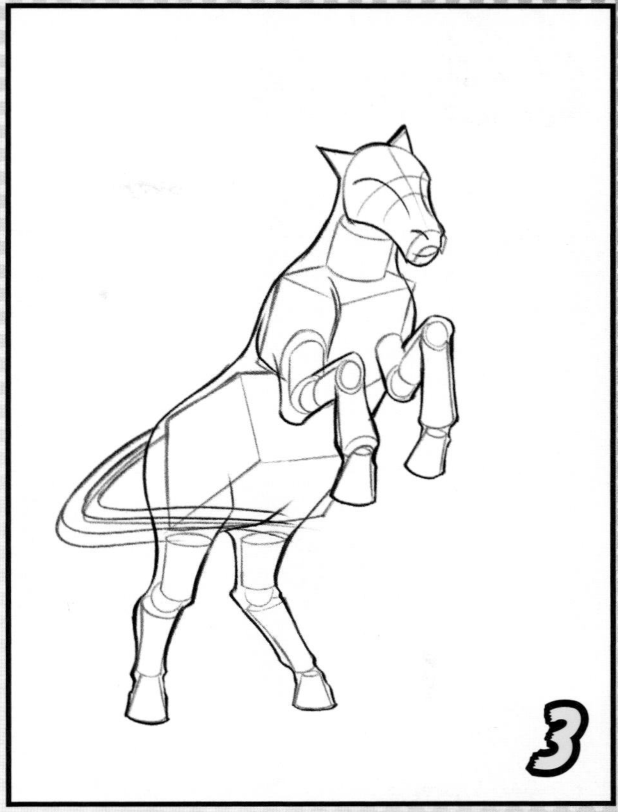
3
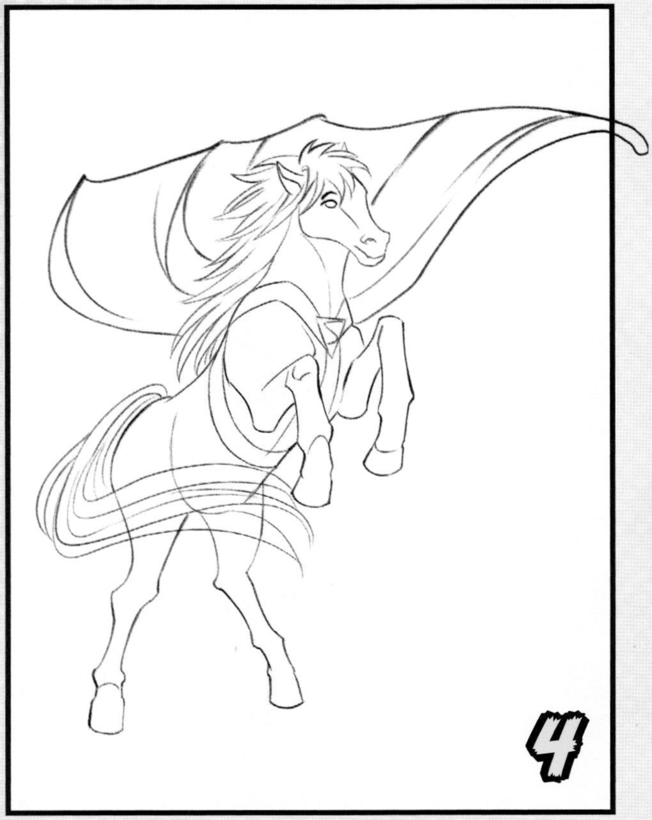
4
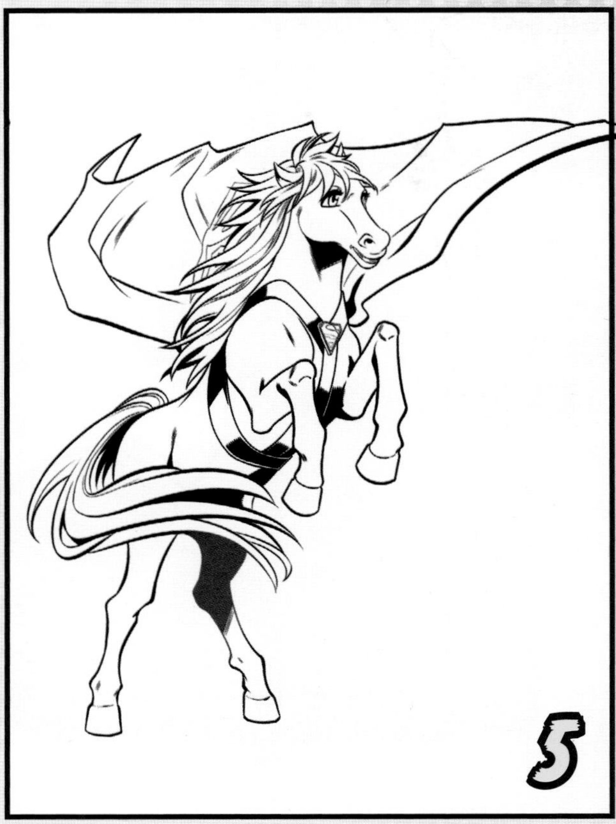
5

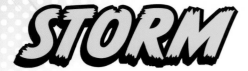

STORM

Whether cutting through currents or weaving through waves, Storm is a wonder to behold. But Aquaman's trusty steed packs more than aquatic horsepower. Just like the King of Atlantis, the super-smart seahorse can also speak to other sea creatures using his mind. With this talent, Storm can call on his friends to help burst the bubbles of black-hearted baddies!

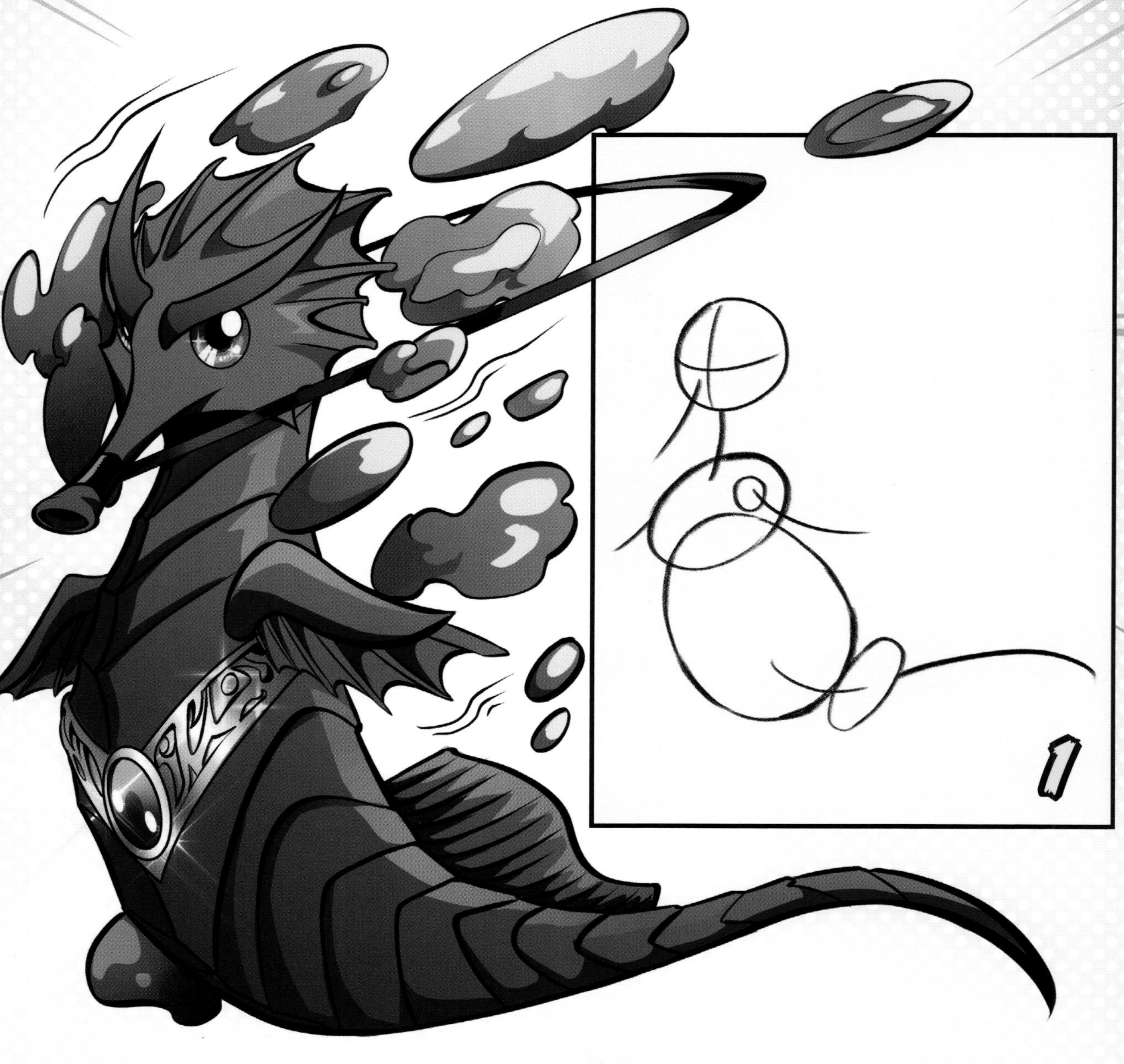
1

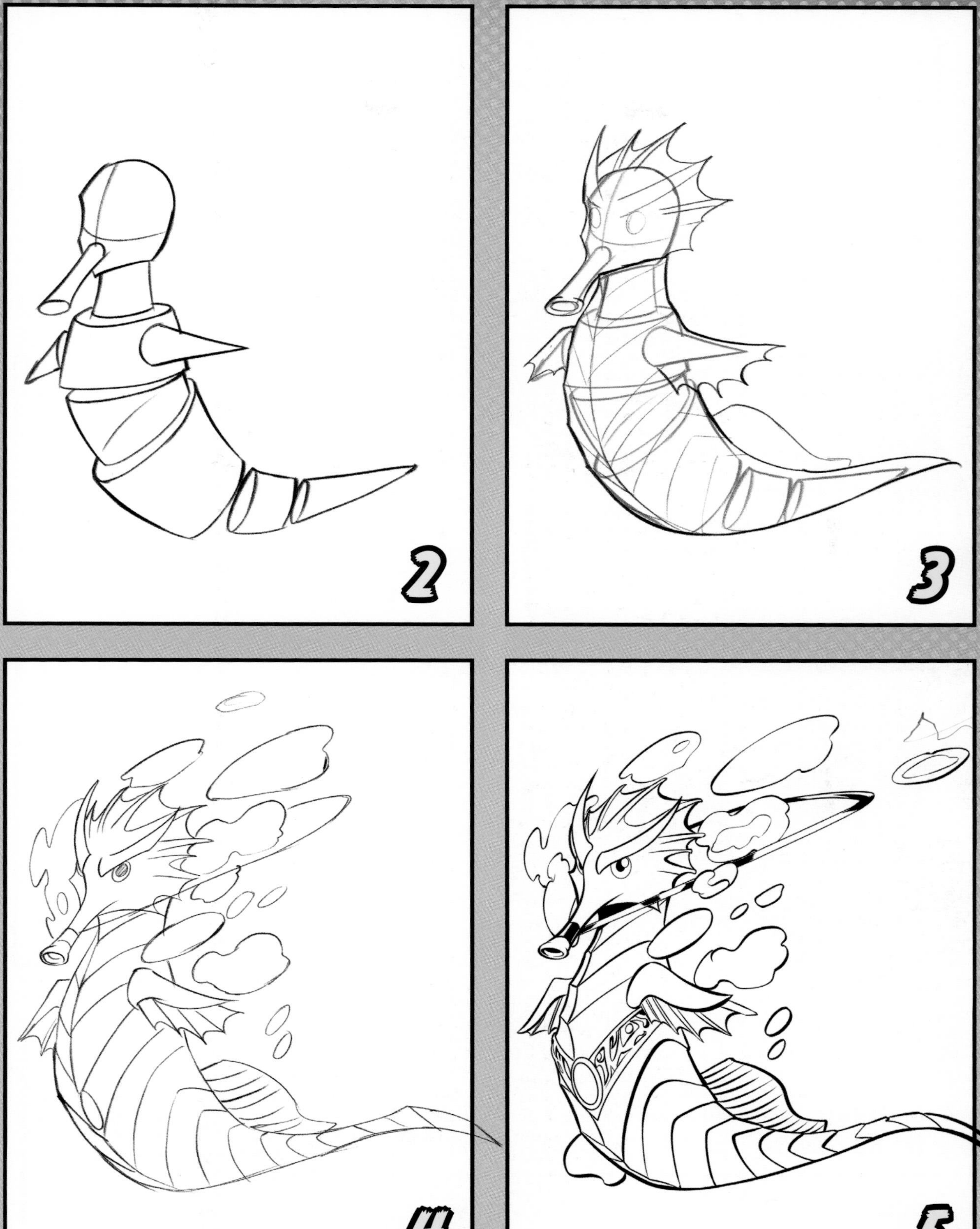
2
3
4
5

WHATZIT

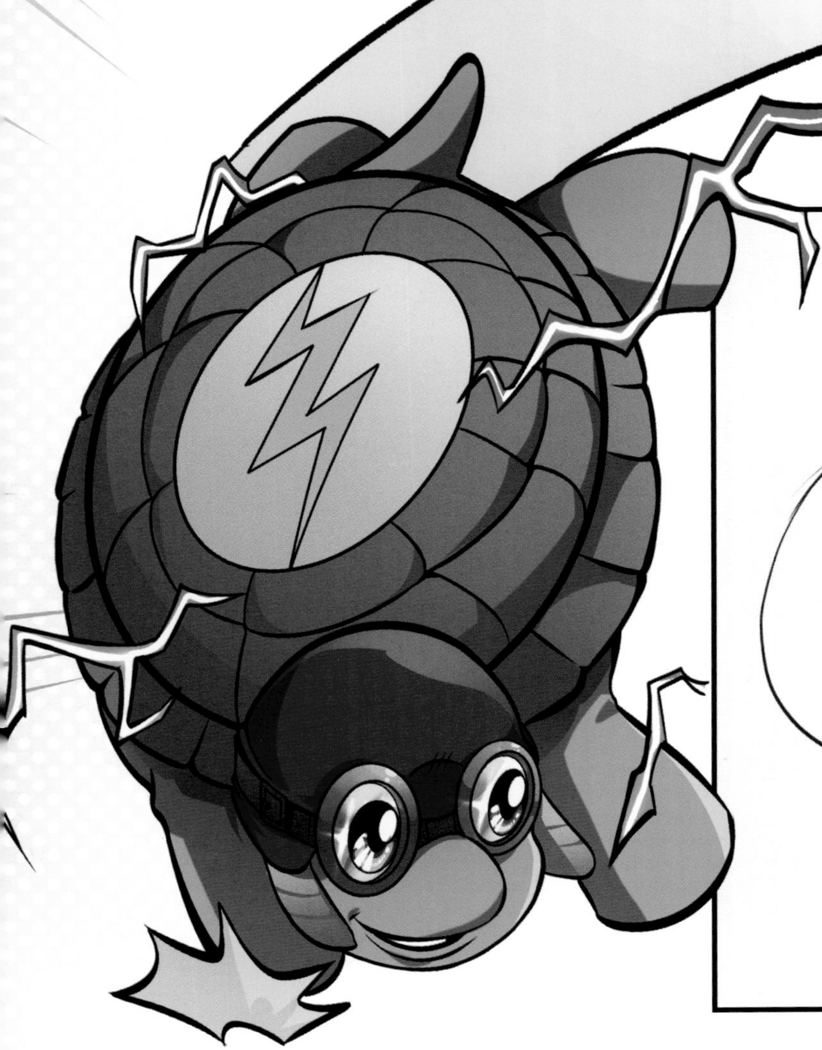

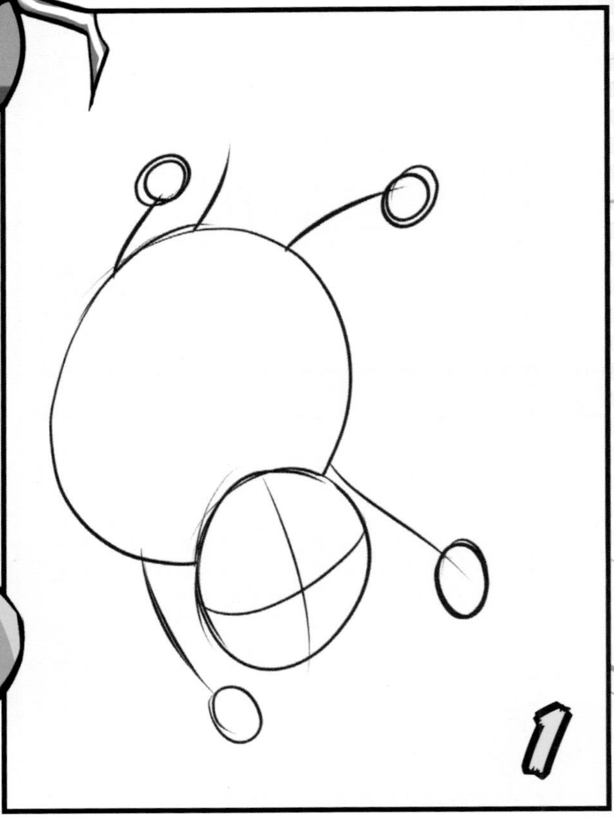
1

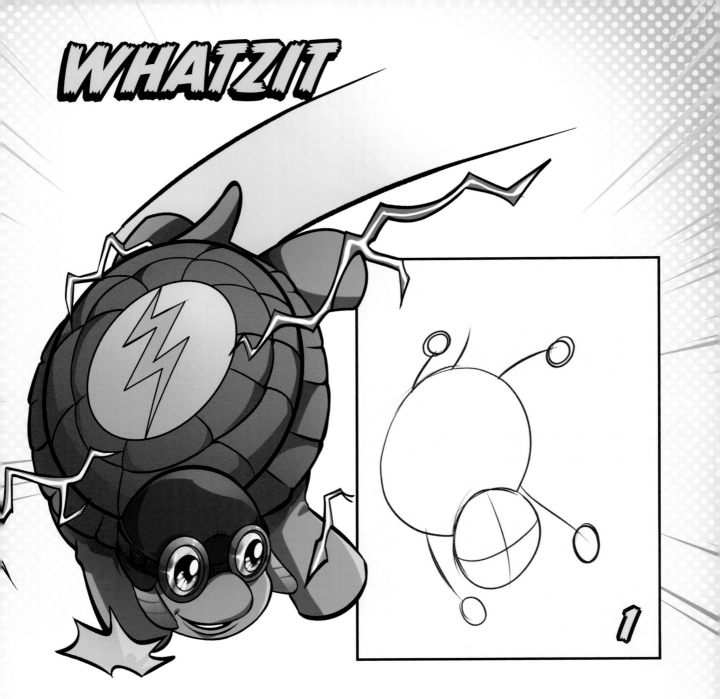

Merton McSnurtle is no ordinary turtle—he's The Fastest Turtle Alive! Better known as Whatzit, this fleet-footed friend of The Flash uses his powers to protect Central City. And what remarkable powers! His connection to the Speed Force is so strong, he can spin up tornadoes that leave enemies shell-shocked.

MANGA FACT

Whatzit's speed lines add a dynamic sense of motion. But these lines are also used in manga to emphasize a character's emotion, such as shock or excitement.

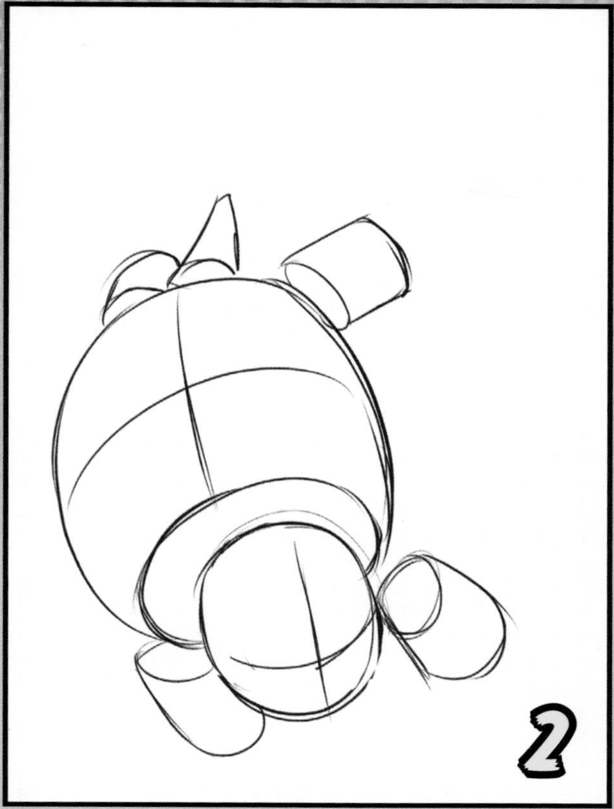
2

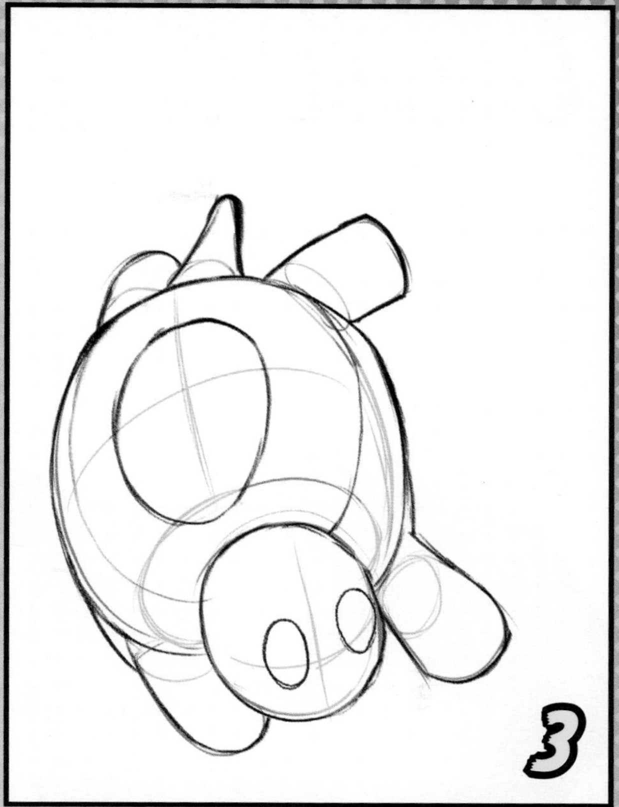
3

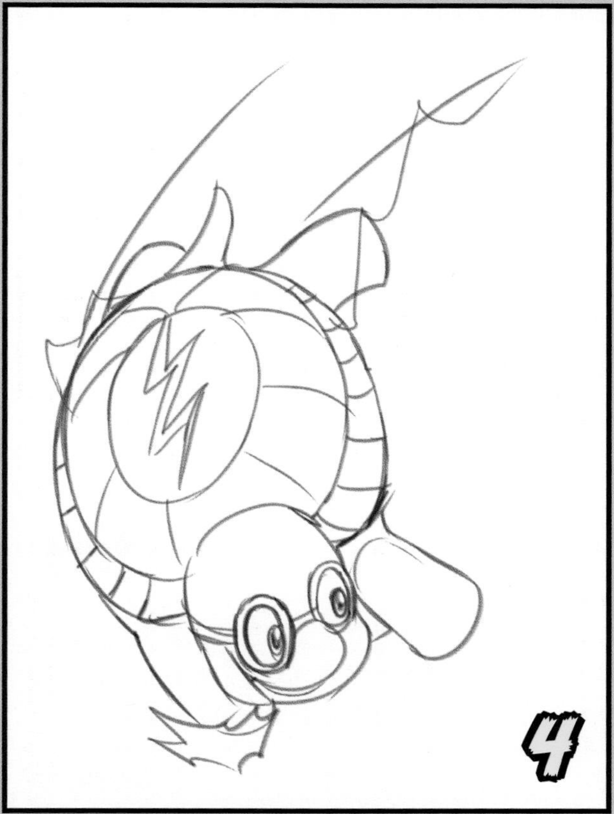
4

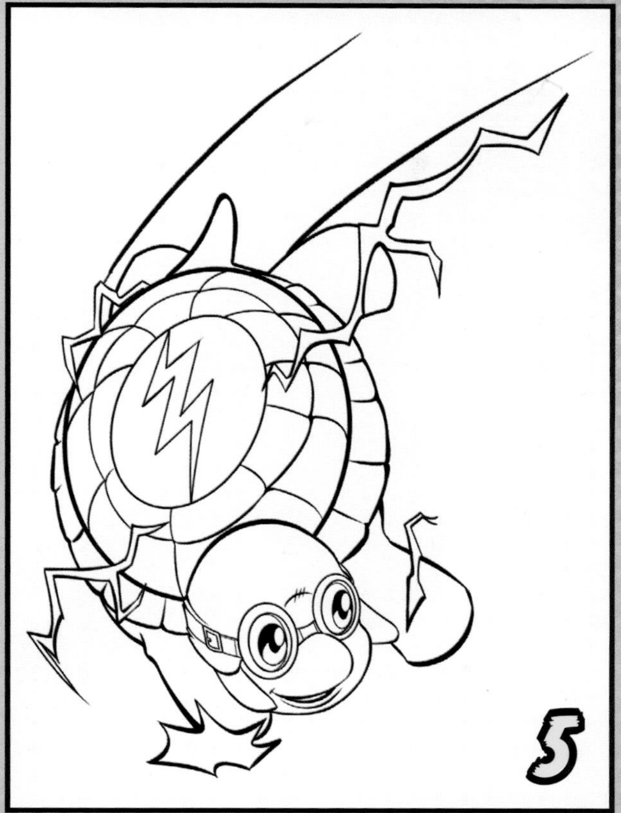
5

BEPPO

Beppo is one mischievous Super-Monkey. Before planet Krypton exploded, he stowed away in Kal-El's rocket ship. Little did he know that the baby would grow up to be Superman! But Beppo was bound for changes too. Once the two Kryptonians arrived on Earth, the yellow sun gave them both superpowers. Now Beppo soars up, up, and away to save the day!

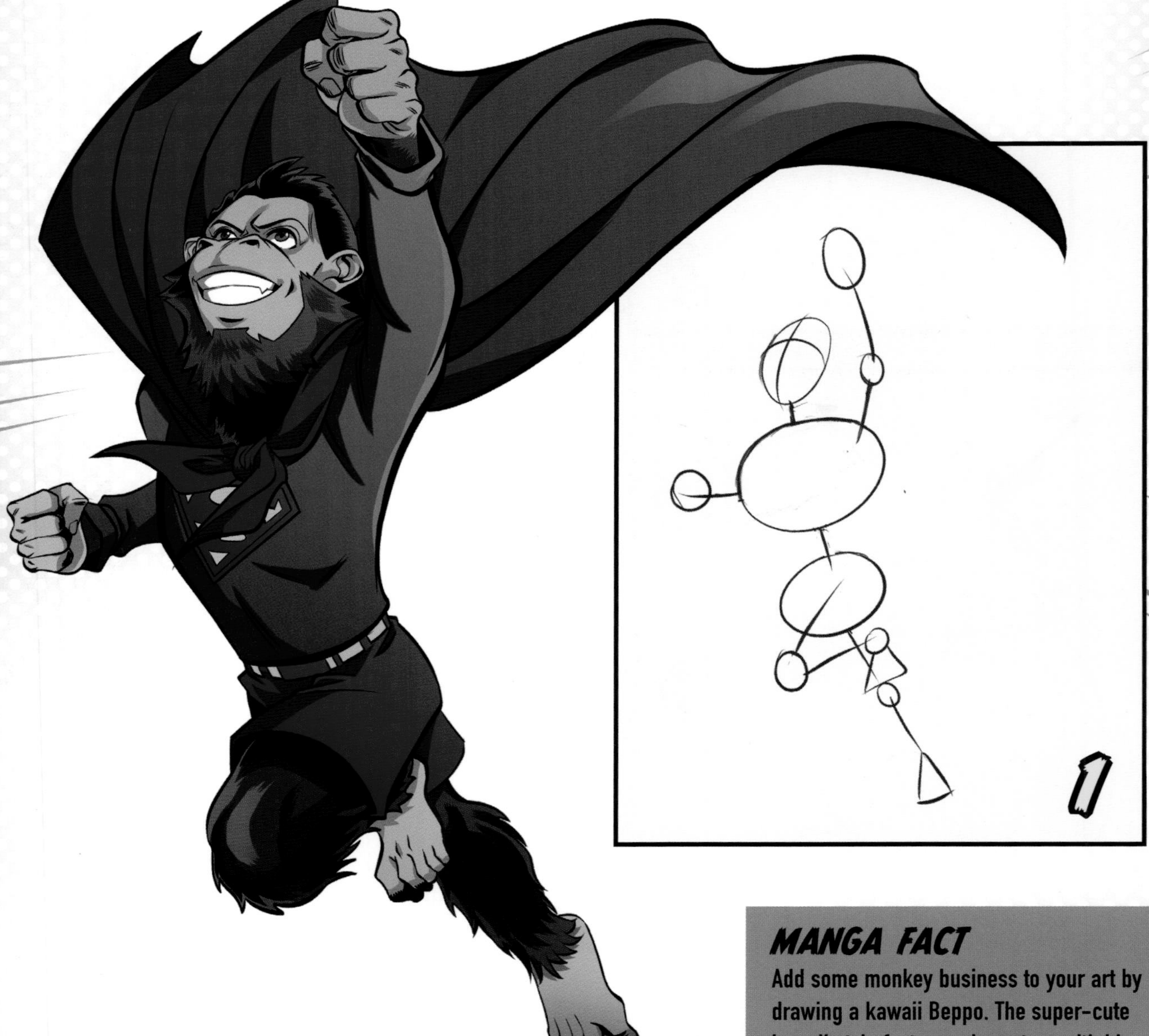
1

MANGA FACT

Add some monkey business to your art by drawing a kawaii Beppo. The super-cute kawaii style features characters with big heads, wide-set eyes, and small bodies.

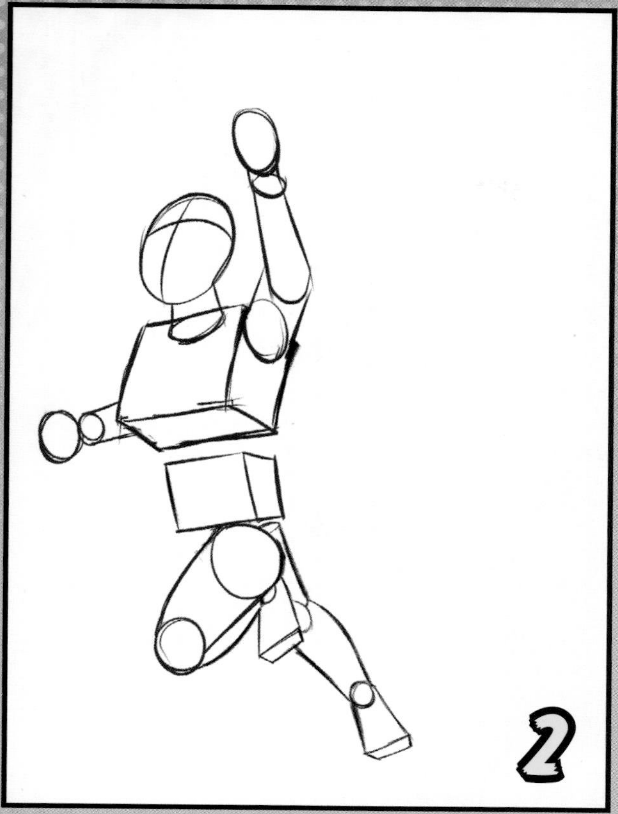
2
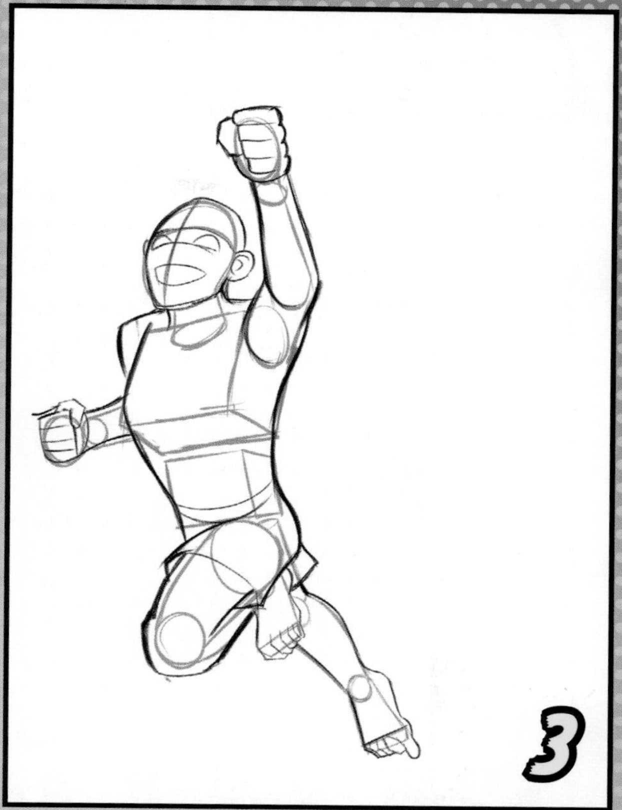
3
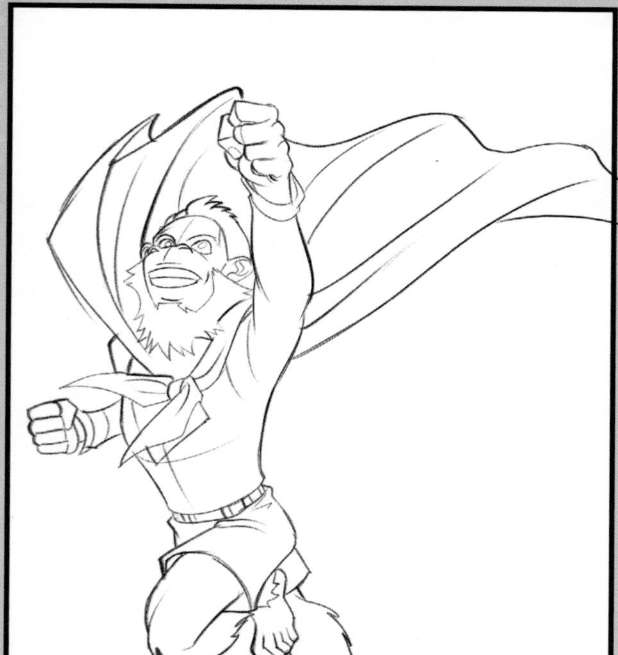
4
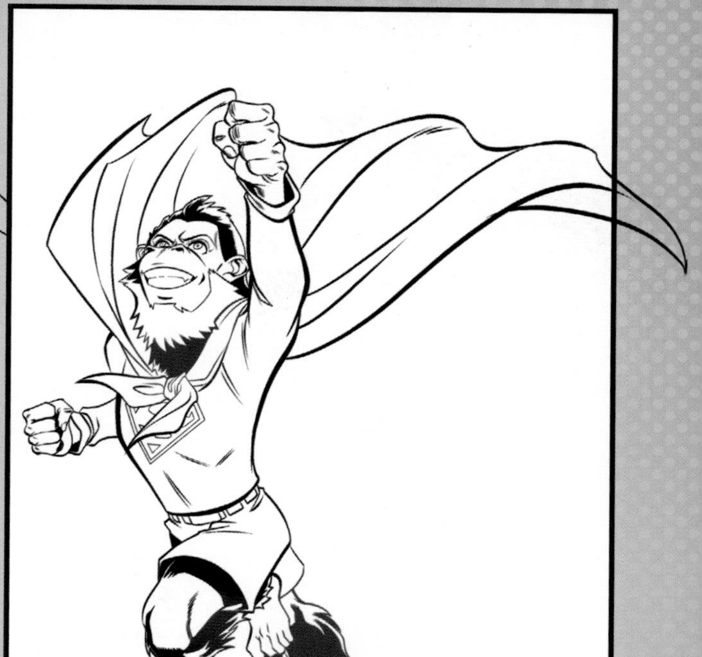
5

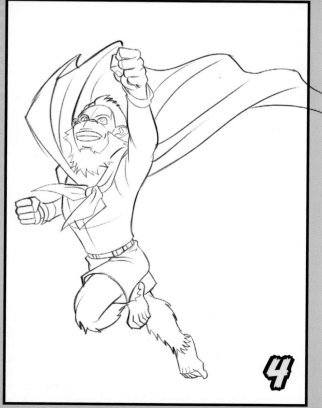

CRACKERS AND GIGGLES

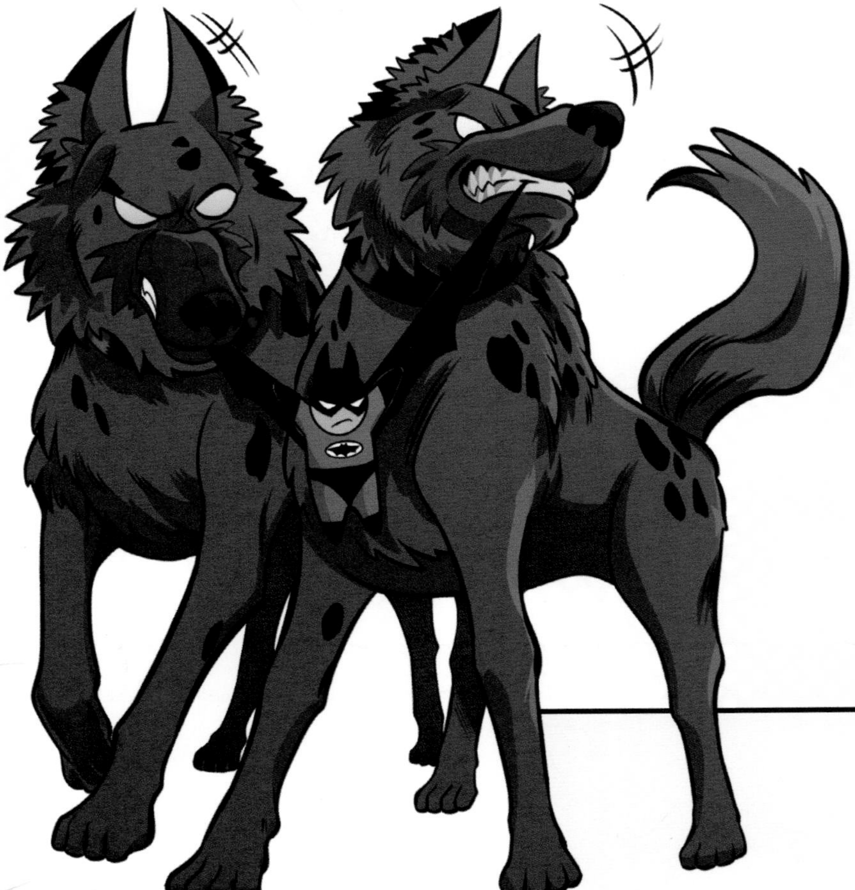

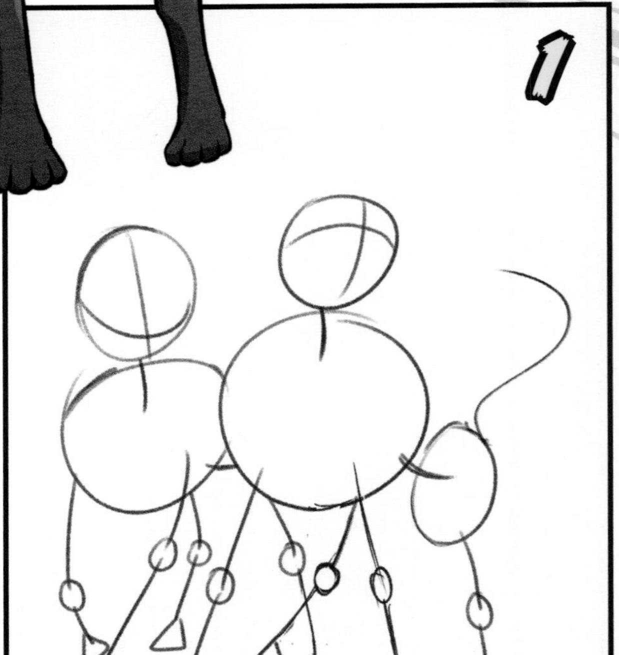
1

Few Super-Villain pets tickle the funny bone quite like Crackers and Giggles. Harley Quinn's two fiendish fur babies often show their loyalty by pulling pranks during her madcap capers. But don't let the hyenas' hilarious hijinks fool you. Given the chance, they would love to take a bite out of Batman!

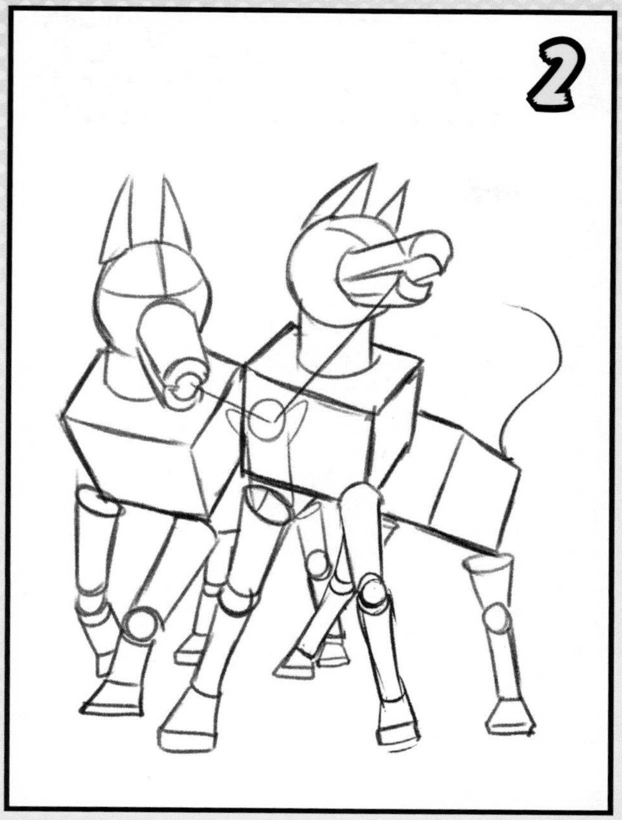
2

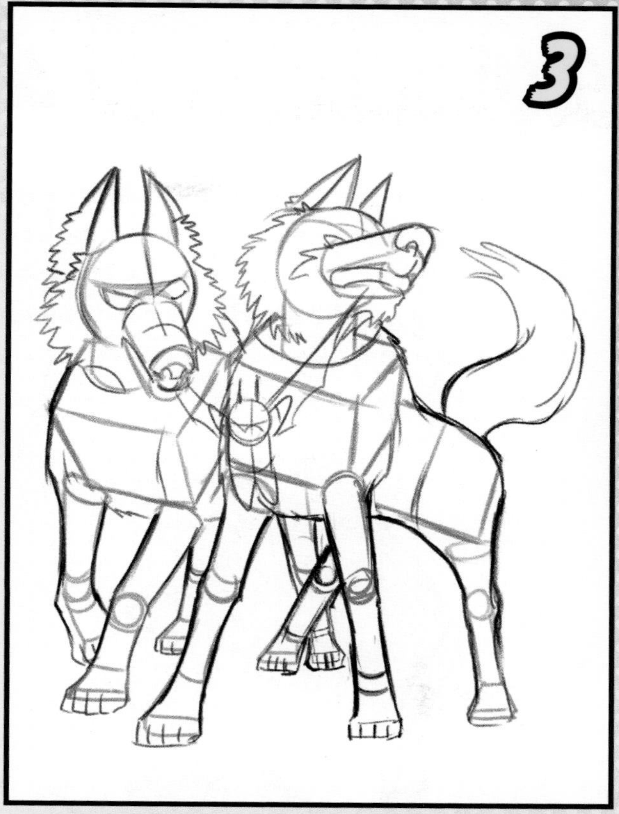
3

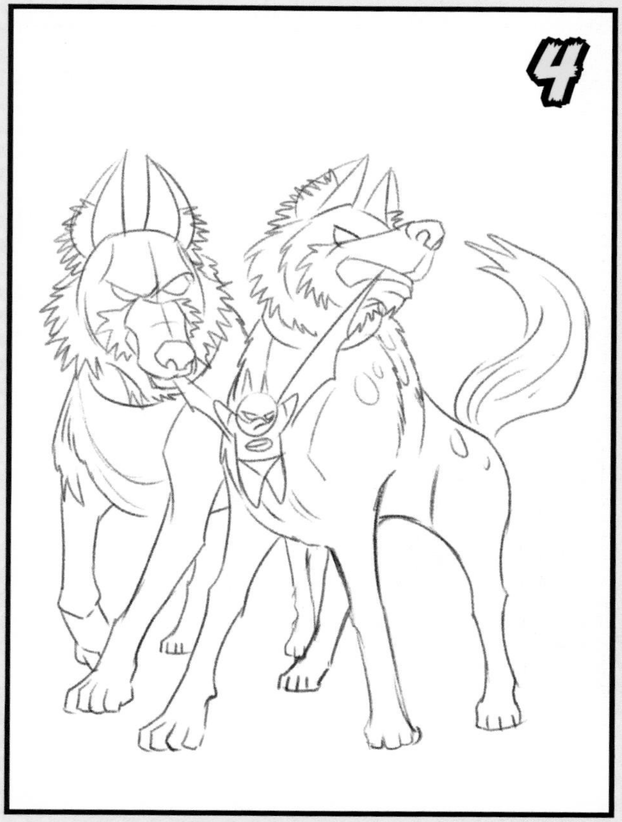
4

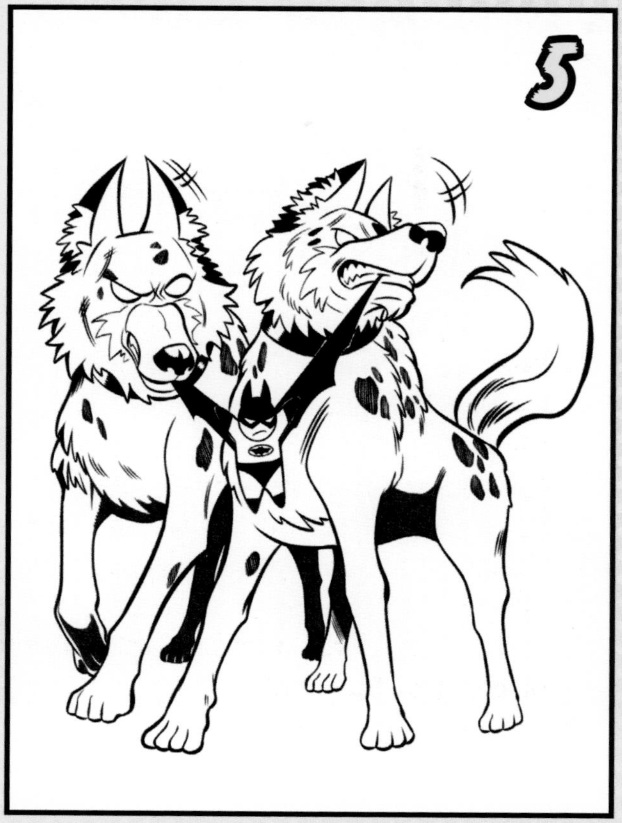
5

IGNATIUS

Leave it to Lex Luthor to have a pet as cold-blooded as himself. Ignatius is an iguana you don't want to meet on the dark streets of Metropolis. This vile reptile is superintelligent and a master of technology. Take extra care if the crook has a chunk of Kryptonite in his clutches. He'll use it to KO any Kryptonian he comes across!

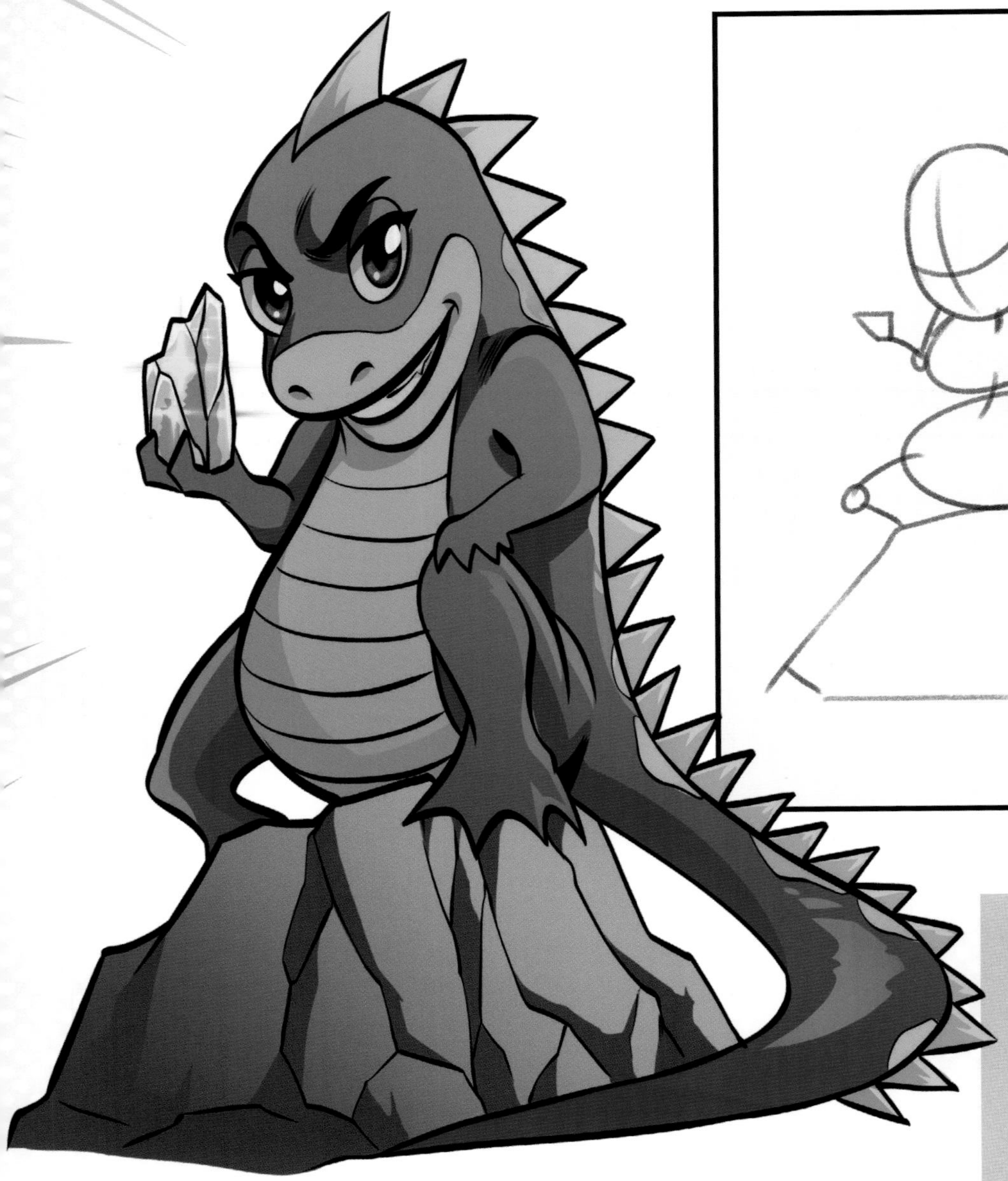

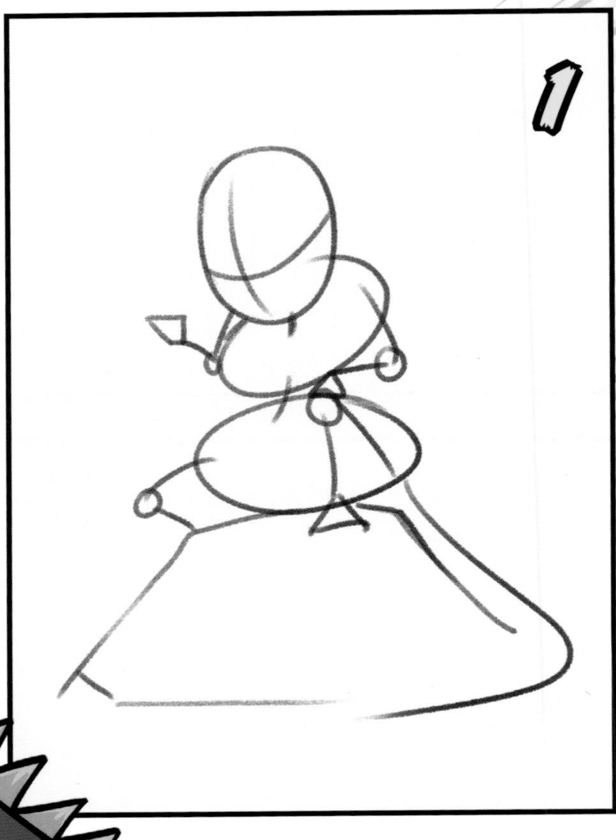
1

MANGA FACT

Manga animals don't always wear clothes. So their personalities often shine through physical features instead. Capture Ignatius's wickedness by showcasing his slithery tail, sharp spines, and evil grin.

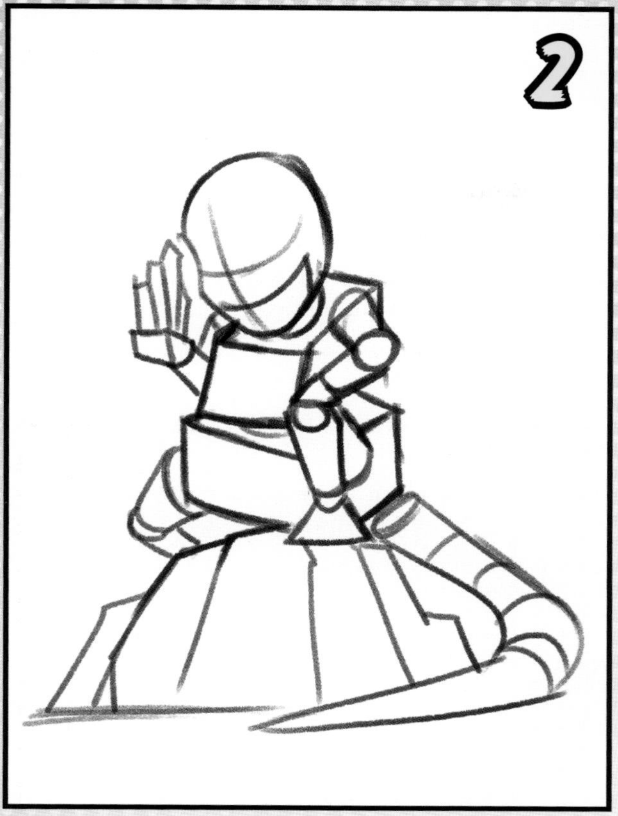
2

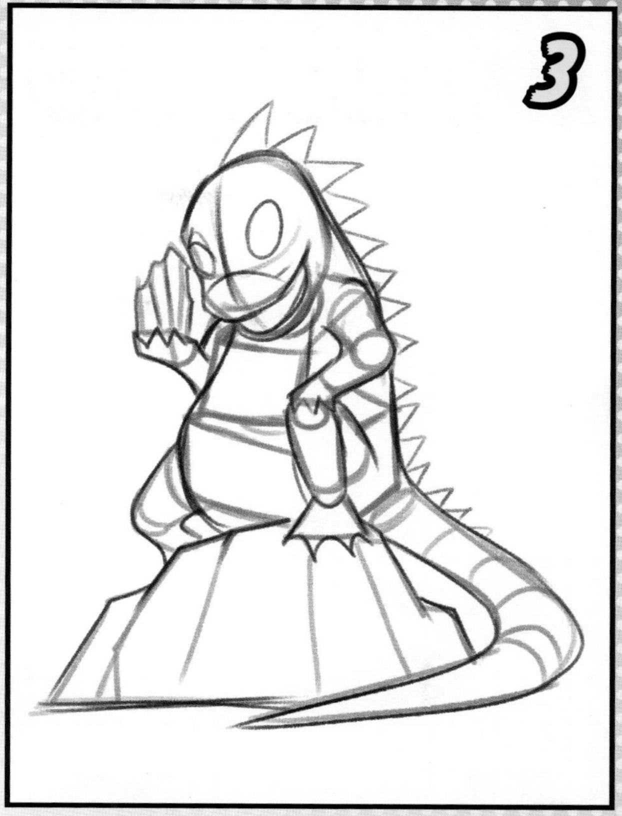
3

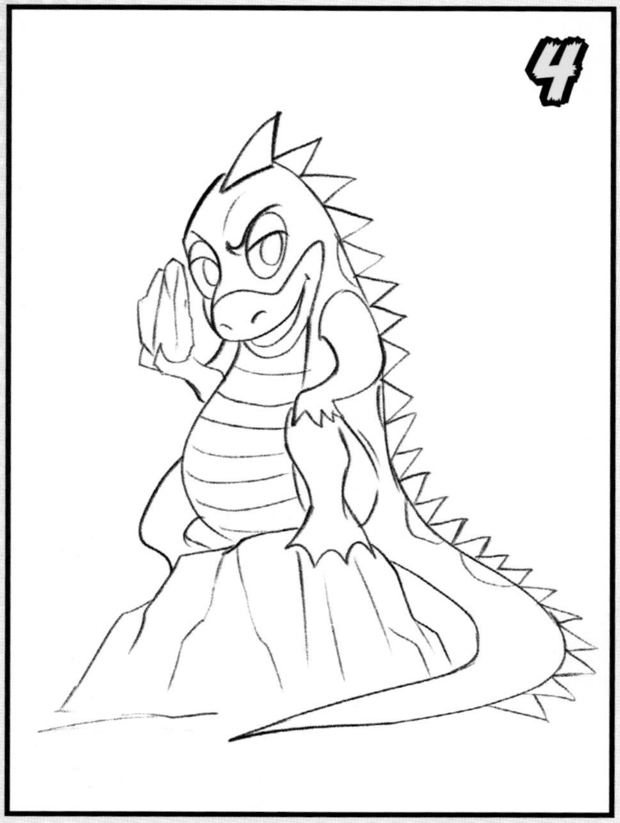
4

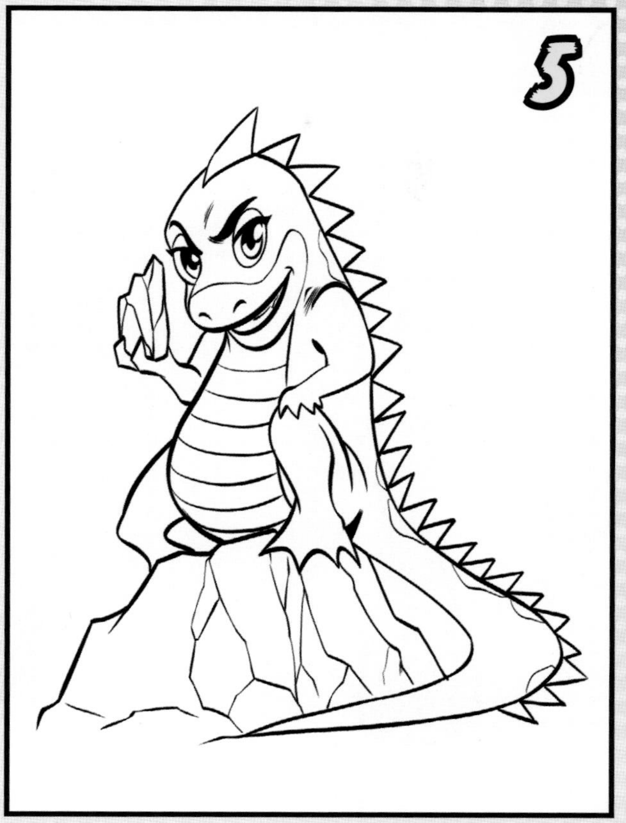
5

DOGWOOD

When Poison Ivy wanted a pet, she did what any floral felon would do. The Queen of Green used her skills to combine a dog with a plant! The result was the dastardly Dogwood. The horrible hybrid can control trees with his mind and has a bite that's worse than his bark!

MANGA FACT

Japan has manga cafés, or manga kissa. Here people can enjoy coffee and other beverages while reading their favorite manga borrowed from the café's large library.

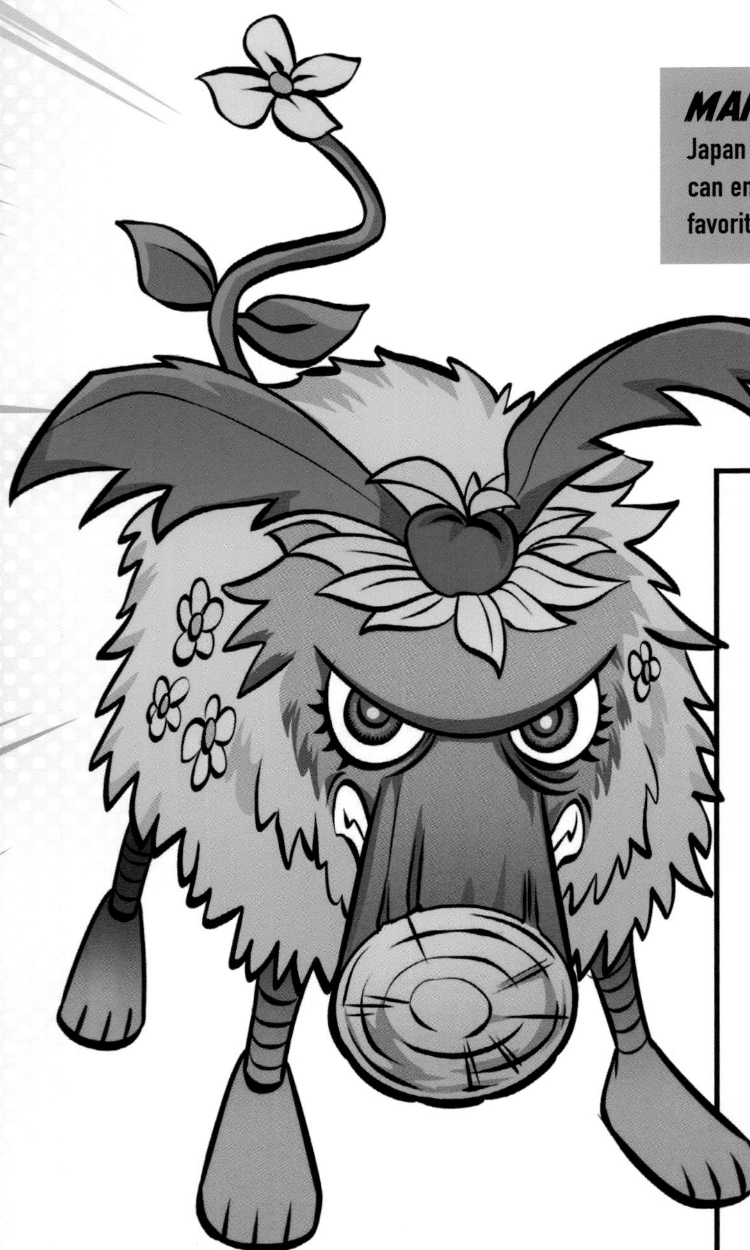

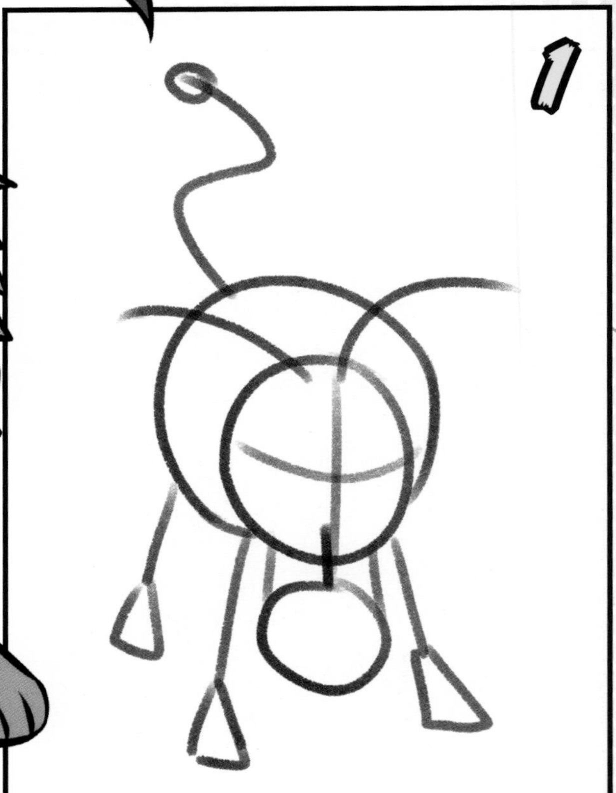
1

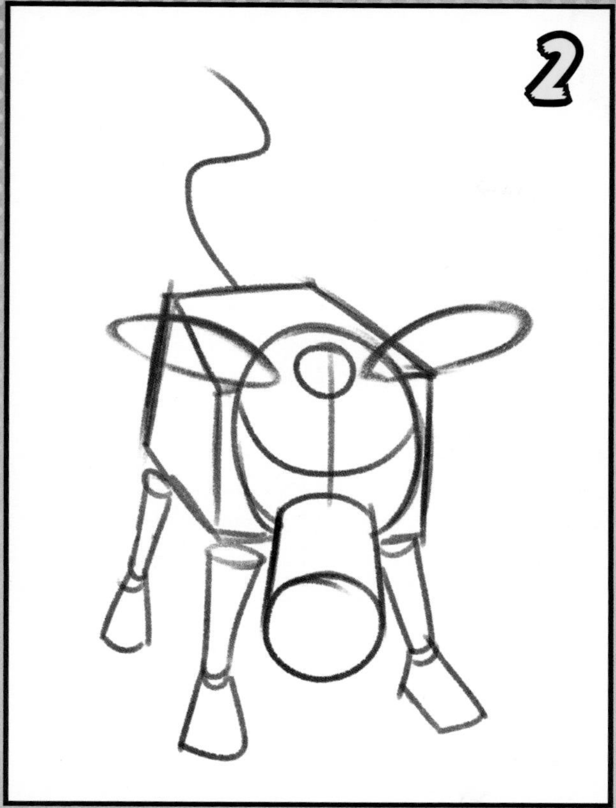
2
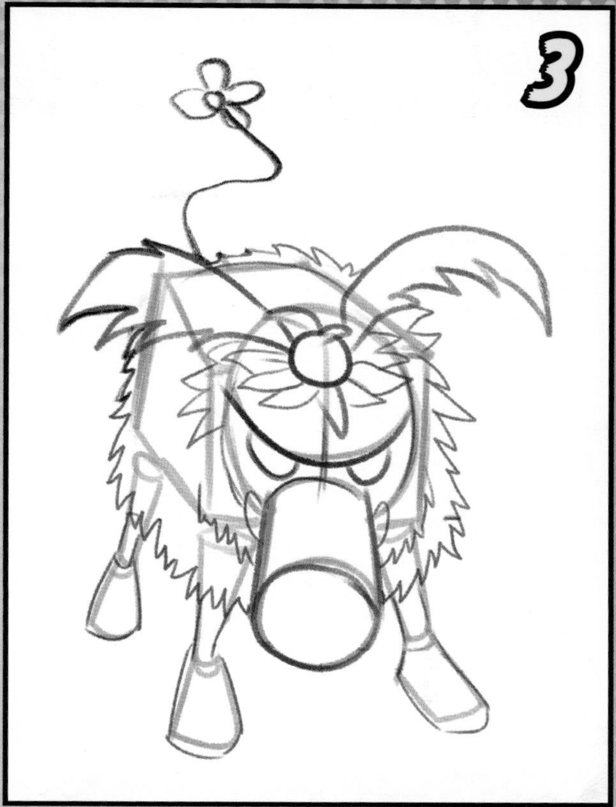
3
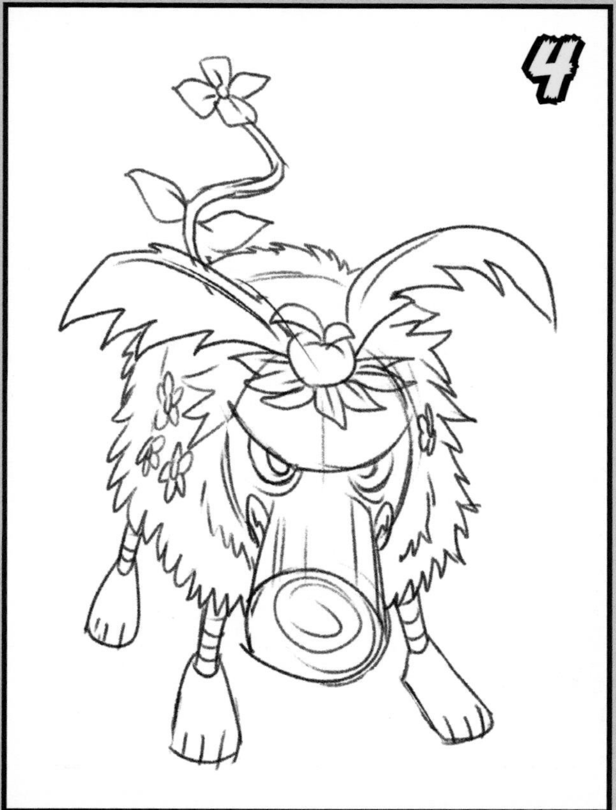
4
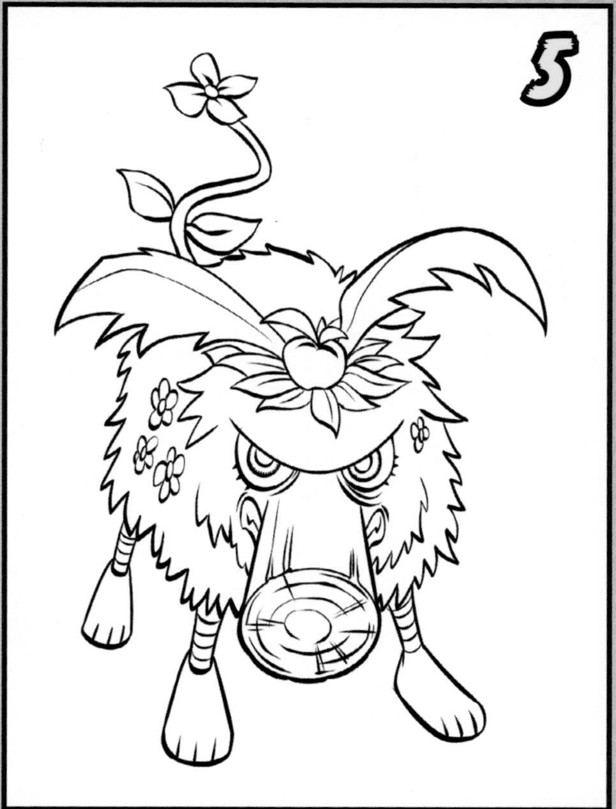
5

B'DG VS. DEX-STARR

High above Earth, a wild battle of wills rages! Green Lantern B'dg uses his green power ring against the red power ring of Red Lantern Dex-Starr. Can the space squirrel corral the corrupt kitty in the coils of justice? Or will the feline fiend cut through the Super Hero's last line of defense? YOU'RE THE MANGAKA. THE FATE OF THE PLANET IS IN YOUR HANDS!

MANGA FACT
Legendary manga creator Osamu Tezuka featured many animals in his stories. One of his most famous is Unico. This super-cute unicorn starred in his own manga from 1976 to 1979.

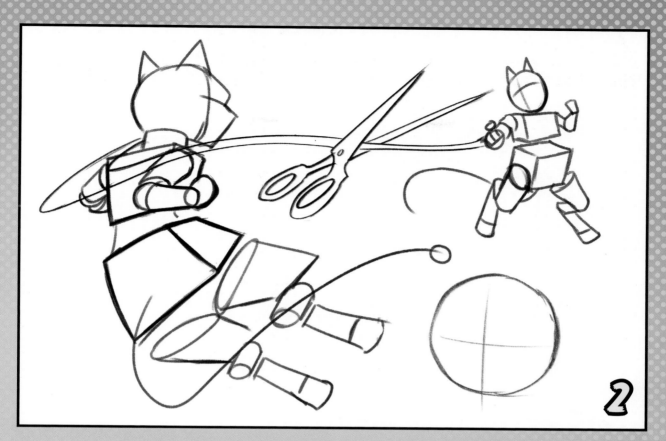

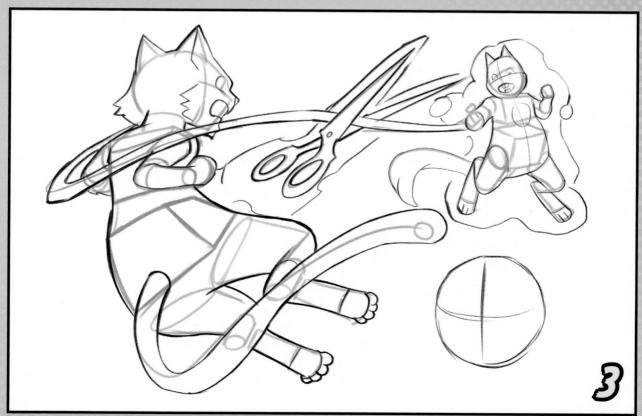

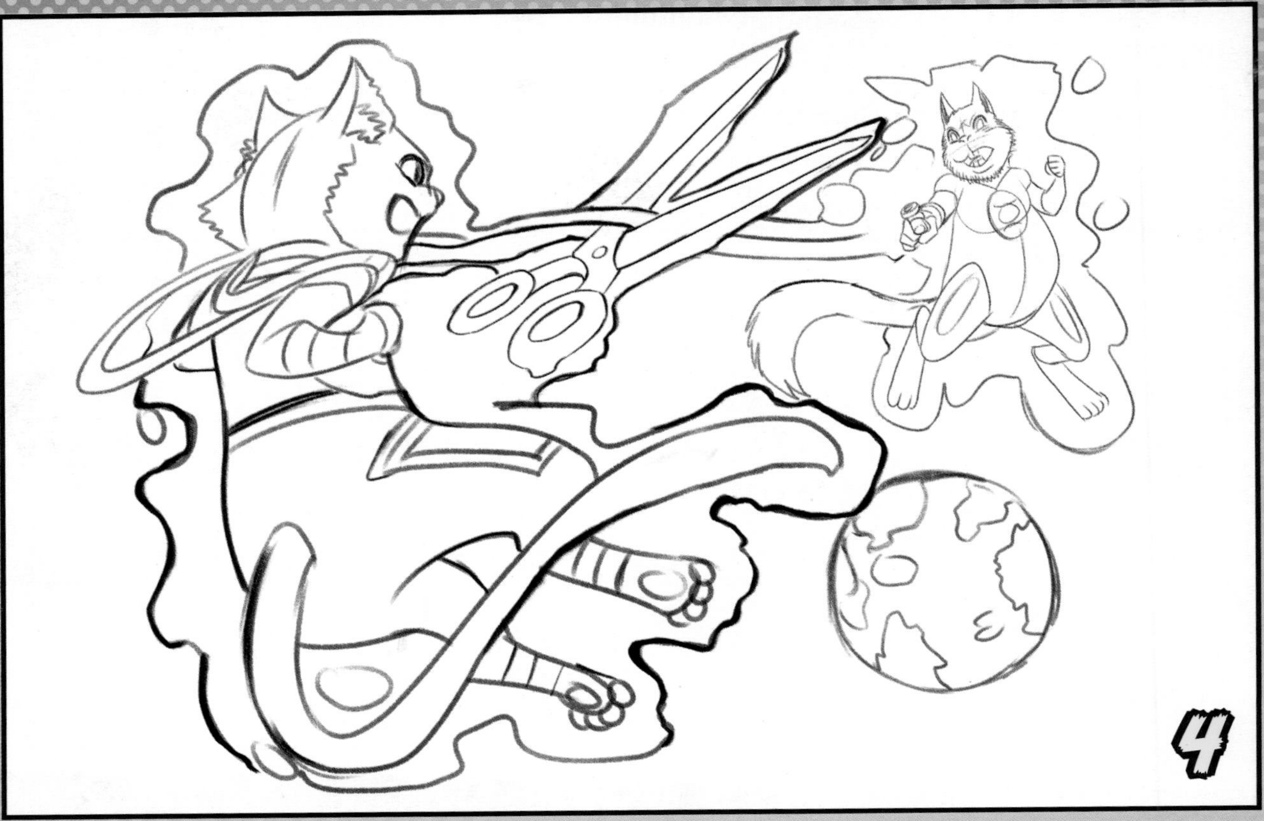
4

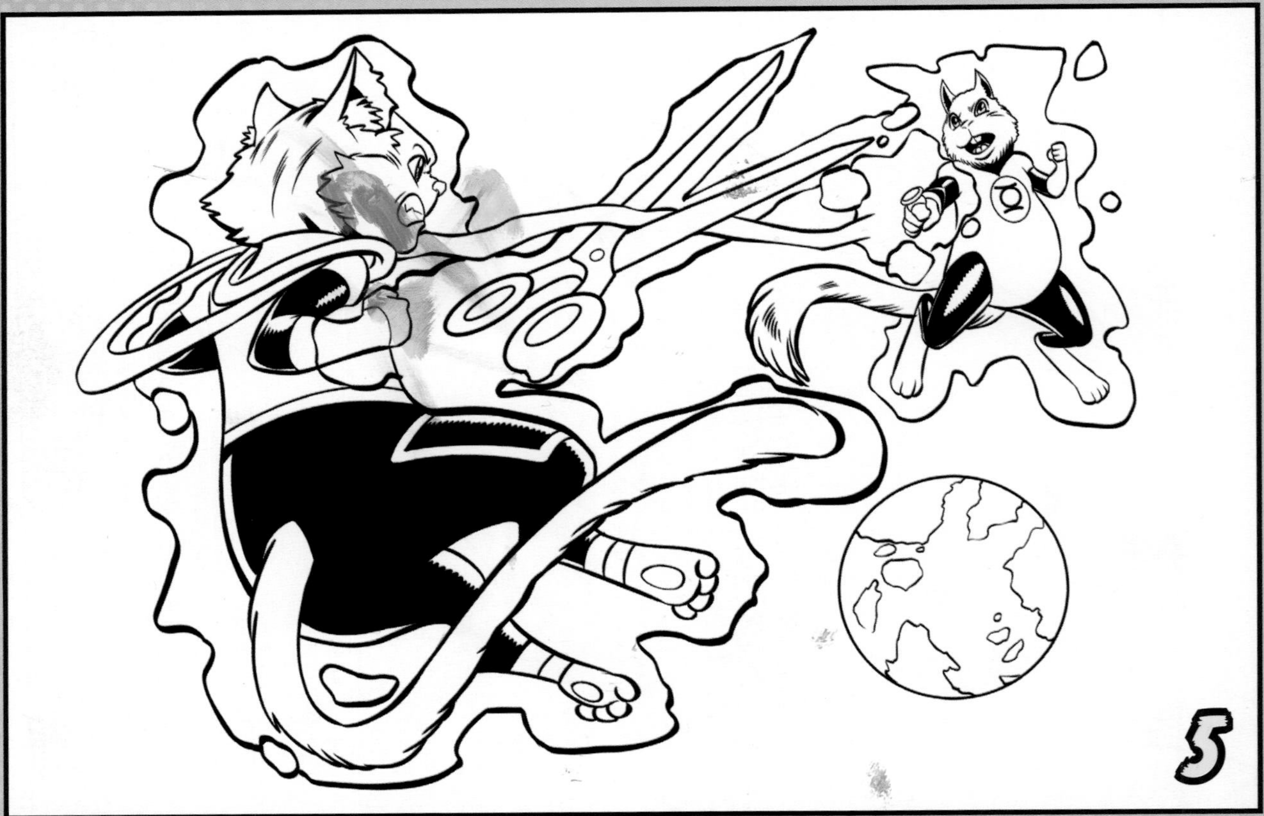
5

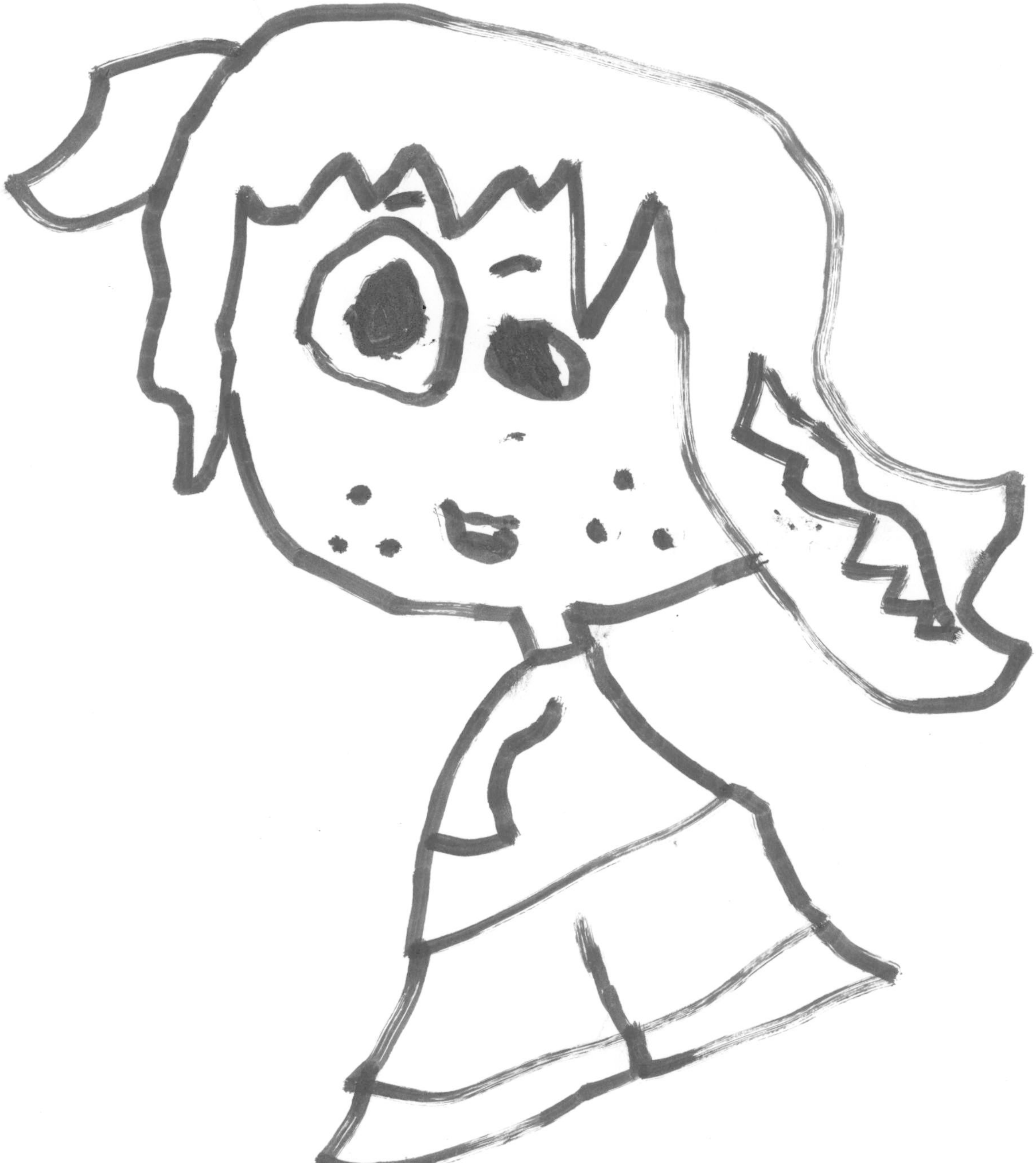

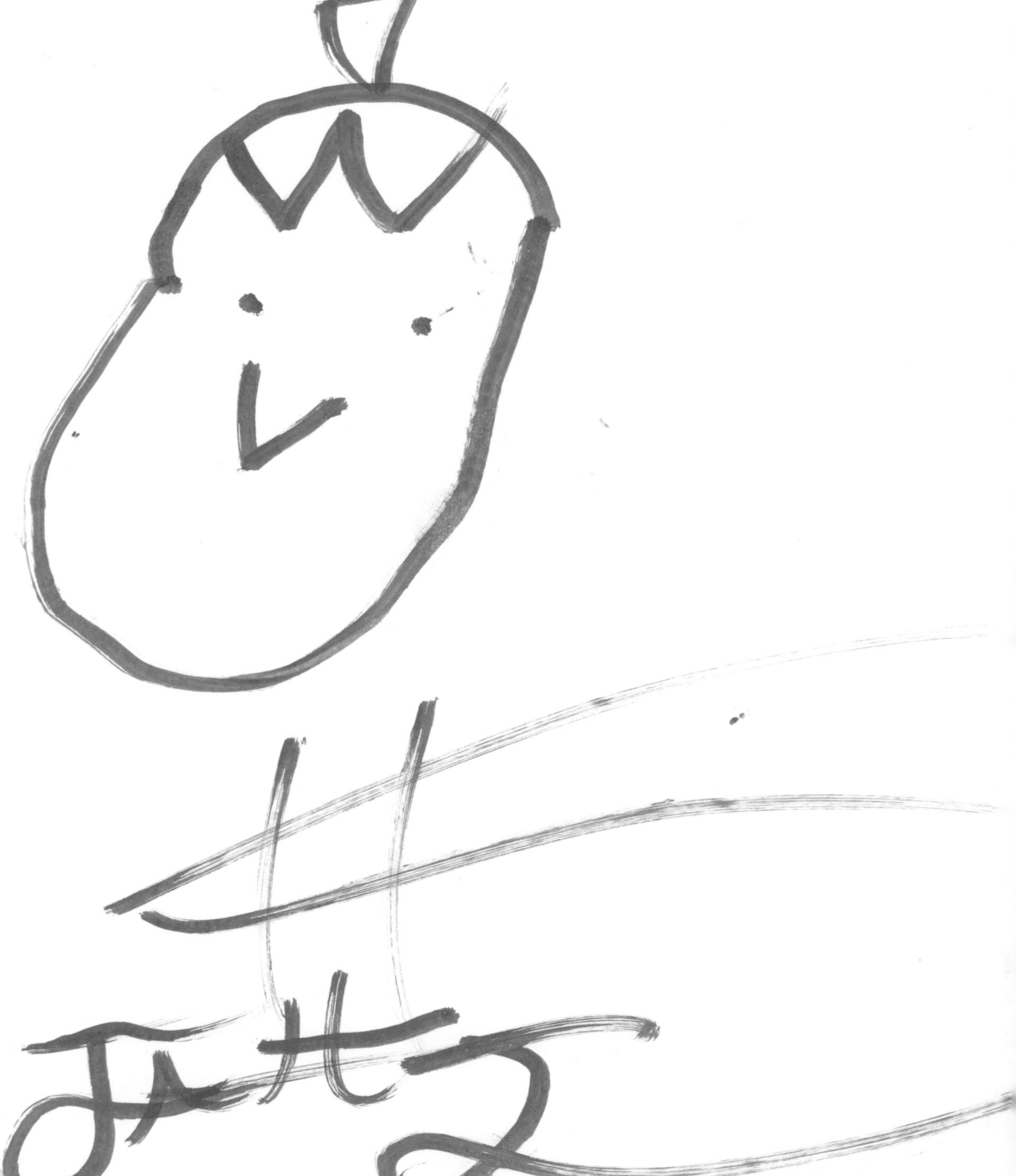